*The Trustworthiness*
*of the Gospels*

# The Trustworthiness
# of the Gospels

HUGO STAUDINGER

Paderborn

*Translated by*
Robin T. Hammond

1981

The Handsel Press

Published by
The Handsel Press Ltd.
33 Montgomery Street, Edinburgh

ISBN 0 905312 15 5


First published 1981

Title of the original German edition
Die historische Glaubwürdigkeit der Evangelien.
Fourth revised edition 1977 published by the Schriftenmissions-Verlag Gladbeck
and the Verlag J. W. Naumann Würzburg.

Printed in Great Britain by
Clark Constable Ltd., Edinburgh

# Contents

*Quotations from the Bible are taken from The New English Bible*
*The titles of books in German are given as published*

# Preliminary reflections

Christianity and the Bible form the focus of many present-day intellectual discussions. Radio and television, illustrated journals and newspapers report on these topics in a detail which at first appears to be astounding. They are not matters of a dispute between learned theologians but of the whole of the faithful, and even people who can hardly be described as believers are drawn into the controversy and mobilized for the one or the other point of view.

Some of those taking part are convinced that religion is a thing of the past and that the Bible is untrustworthy. They are of the opinion that Christianity has indeed played a role in the development of European culture, that its hour glass has run out and it must make way for more progressive philosophies of life.

Other people maintain that there will always be Christianity, also in the future. The message of Jesus must be interpreted differently to the way it was in past centuries. The fulfilment of the teaching of Jesus consists in social and political engagement. God is a cipher for fellowship and humanity. He always fits in where we turn positively to mankind. He is a symbol of imminent worldly acts, in the spirit of love and not a guarantee of hope in the world to come.

On the other hand there are Christians who are of the opinion that the message of Jesus will be betrayed and Christianity abandoned as a result of these movements. In order to defend the true and pure Gospel they have banded together and now demand that a clear line should be drawn between teaching and false teaching.

This situation is a challenge to the Churches, to believers, and to theologians. The Church leaders are hardly able to hinder a breaking up into various wings.

In this situation the question can well be asked, 'What has the historian to do with these matters?' 'Shouldn't he be clever and stay out of the whole affair, instead of getting himself mixed up in the disputes of theology, which is another discipline?' But this piece of advice does not meet reality. Anyone who follows the learned discussion closely is forced to the conclusion that almost all theologians claim to be working with critical historical methods.

The history specialist notes however that many — amongst whom are known and unknown theologians — handle historical methods in quite an unconstrained manner, and reach conclusions which seem peculiarly strange. The historian can only shake his head at much which has apparently been worked out by historical methods, and in a manner which at first glance might seem ingenious.

In the last few years, however, a number of discussions have taken place between historians and theologians, which have since been published by the Deutsches Institut für Bildung und Wissen in its series of major works.[1] In contrast to the theologians, the historians of various denominations and leanings were astonishingly united over many questions, so that they may perhaps be in a position to help towards their solution.

The statements and expositions which follow have been set down with this in mind. Since they first appeared they have caused so much interest that a second, a third, and a fourth edition were necessary. For each new edition I worked over the text again, sometimes adding to it, and sometimes shortening it. As the book has stood the test of four editions it seems only reasonable that the work should be published in English.

The investigation which follows is devoted to the question, 'What can historical scholarship say about the credibility of the New Testaments writings, using its own historical methods?' Theological questions have therefore only been touched upon. Theological literature has only been drawn into the deliberations in so far as the works make or assert historical statements in order to argue historically. In order to avoid confusion by the presentation of too many points of view the dispute with the theologians is mainly limited to Rudolf Bultmann, who is the

1 Deutsches Institut für Bildung und Wissen: ed. Ascher, Paul, Evangelium und Geschichte in einer rationalisierten Welt, Trier 1969; Deutsches Institut für Bildung und Wissen: ed. Hollenbach, J. M. und Staudinger, Hugo, Moderne Exegese und historische Wissenschaft, Trier 1972.

distinguished exponent of the demythologizing school of theology, and Willi Marxsen, who has won a high degree of influence, especially in Germany. This limitation has had the effect that more recent exegetic publications have not been considered which have shown in part a greater balance and an earnest desire to do justice to the historicity of events. Another result is that I must also renounce reference to a number of theological publications in which my reflections, which were first put forward in 1969, have already found a positive consideration.

Before I close these preliminary reflections I wish to thank my friends and colleagues in the Deutsches Institut für Bildung und Wissen, especially Heinrich Kraft and Peter Bläser for their critical comments and valuable suggestions.

For the English edition I owe special thanks to Thomas Torrance, who gave me the initial encouragement, and Robin Hammond, who undertook the difficult task of translation.

# 1. The presentation and testimony of Jesus of Nazareth according to the New Testament

When the historian begins to consider the man called Jesus he faces a number of difficulties. The main difficulty lies in the special nature of the person, Jesus himself; that is if he is considered and accepted as described in the Gospels, and also in view of the impossibility of forming a picture of him without resort to the Gospels.

If one begins with the accounts given in the Gospels, then a unique claim or postulate is put forward. Jesus of Nazareth is described as *the* Son of God. Unfortunately this description has become so accepted and so familiar within the Christian tradition, that we do not take exception to it, and hardly sense a trace of the unheard of nature of this statement. One proof of this is the way in which we celebrate Advent. It is so presented as if the whole of mankind, or at least all the Jews in the Old Testament, are waiting for the promised Son of God.

It would be taking matters too far to ask whether one can speak of the expectations of the *whole of mankind*. The Jews, from whom Jesus comes, have to some extent waited for a promised Messiah, certainly not for 'the Son' of Jehovah. In the Old Testament there is the designation 'Son of God' not only for the people of Israel but also for characters individually chosen by God. Nevertheless there is never the thought of a full and true filial relationship to God, as appears in the writings of the New Testament.

The Jewish scholar Schalom Ben-Chorin quite rightly underlines the· fact, 'The claim with which he (Jesus) comes forward went far beyond all that old Israel expected from the Promised One ... We do not know a Son of God and do not expect him in the future, but we know once and for all that we are all 'children of the living God', and that he is our Father and King ... God remains God from the Jewish point of view, and Man

1

remains Man; even the Messiah, if he is expected, is conceived of as a man of flesh and blood, not as a Son being of one substance with the Father, 'wholly God and wholly Man' as the dogma states. Israel acknowledged and acknowledges, and as long as a Jew still breathes will continue to acknowledge 'Hear, O Israel, the Lord our God, the Lord is one'. How should the Son be set in this Unity with the Father, let alone being completed by a third person, the Holy Ghost? That is again a supposition which Hebrew thinking cannot conceive and will not conceive, because the true oneness and unity of God, the inviolable 'Eschad' would thereby be violated in a sacrilege which is inconceivable to us.'[2]

Naturally one can and must point out that the expression 'of one substance with the Father' is not formulated in this way in the writings of the New Testament. Nonetheless one should not allow oneself to be led astray by this fact, as the claim already mentioned is raised in the writings of the New Testament through many precise wordings and the drawing of analogies. On account of this claim Jesus was a source of anger to the Jews and was, according to the testimony of the New Testament writings, delivered up to Pilate.

Since the unique claim of Jesus is not covered by the Jewish expectations, it can be stated with certainty that the Jews — also the Apostles and the Disciples of Jesus — did not invent this claim. This statement applies also to Paul. It is inconceivable that Paul, raised in the strong Jewish tradition, would have dared of his own accord to transform the received Jewish form of monotheism in this way.

Many Christian and non-Christian scholars have tried to make 'Hellenistic influences' responsible for the claim of Jesus to be the Son of God. As opposed to these attempts it cannot be sufficiently stressed that there is a big difference as to whether the heroes and other demi-gods who crop up in Greek myths claim to have a god for a father, or whether the claim is made for Jesus of Nazareth to be the Son of God, since the gods in the Greek myths were gods among the gods in a whole world of the imagination in which there were constant interchanges between gods and people. Over both gods and people reigned Fate, an impersonal, invisible, superior authority.

2 Schalom Ben-Chorin, Jüdische Fragen um Christus (from book Juden, Christen, Deutsche), Stuttgart, third edition 1961, p. 143 ff.

The God, however, whose son was called Jesus is, according to the conviction of both Judaism and Christianity, the sole God of the whole world, who created everything, who through almighty providence holds sway over all, and rule everything, whose thoughts are not the thoughts of ordinary human beings, who is therefore at an immense, irreconcilable distance from human beings. There is no compromise and no transition between the Jewish-Christian and the Greek-Hellenic concept of God.[3] Paul was well aware of this on his mission to the heathens. This is what he writes to the Thessalonians, 'They themselves spread the news of . . . how you turned from idols, to be servants of the living and true God, and to wait expectantly for the appearance from heaven of his Son Jesus, whom he raised from the dead, Jesus our deliverer from the terrors of judgement to come.'[4] Such examples show that the preaching of Jesus' filial relationship to God go hand in hand with the renunciation of the Hellenic world of gods.

The uniqueness of the presentation of Jesus of Nazareth is matched by the uniqueness of the verification expressed with such conviction in the writings of the New Testament. Not only are there reports of a number of his especially impressive deeds, such as are otherwise told only about very unusual men, and founders of a religion, but it is also reported of him that he rose out of his tomb and appeared in person.

In view of the unique statements made in the Gospels, there arises forcibly for the historian the question as to whether that which is reported in the New Testament is credible from the historical point of view.[5]

3 cf. Note 67.
4 1. Thess 1, 9 ff.
5 See Staudinger, Hugo, Gott: Fehlanzeige? Überlegung eines Historikers zu Grenzfragen seiner Wissenschaft, Spee-Verlag Trier, 1968. The theoretical and methodical questions are also dealt with in the study which Wolfgang Behler and I brought out, namely, Chance und Risiko der Gegenwart, Eine kritische Analyse der wissenschaftlich-technischen Welt, Paderborn 1976.

3

## 2. *Dates of composition of the New Testament*

The time lapse between the actual happenings and their establishment in the written form of the New Testament writings is relatively brief. In point of time the Letter to the Thessalonians, which has already been mentioned, and which was written down in Corinth in the year 50 or 51 — not even two decades after the crucifixion — is the oldest document in the New Testament. The latest is the Gospel according to St. John, if one leaves out the Revelations and a few late letters which are not important for the questions under discussion. The Gospel was probably composed in its present form towards the end of the first century.

A very first glance at the available writings must lead to the simple, and yet little appreciated observation, that the quintessence of the Christian message is the announcement of 'God the Father', of 'our Lord Jesus Christ' and of the 'Holy Ghost'; as well as the announcement of the death, of the resurrection, and of the coming again of Jesus; and finally the hope of eternal life for all believers granted thanks to the grace of Christ; all these are to be found in the writings of the New Testament, beginning with the First Letter to the Thessalonians, and going right on to the Gospel according to St. John. These basic truths were established from the beginning and were carefully handed on.

The earliest documents, however, of the New Testament canon, namely the letters of Paul, only give a few indications of specific happenings in the life of Jesus, since they were written in each case for particular reasons to individual communities, and the contents deal with current matters of church organization, with theological, liturgical, or other pastoral matters. The main happenings of the death on the cross and the resurrection of Jesus are thereby mentioned; moreover the other deeds and sayings of Jesus are only reported in a few places and for a particular reason. The most well-known occurrence is the account of the last supper in the First Letter to the Corinthians,

4

which Paul inserts in order to warn against any unseemly celebration of the Lord's Supper.'[6]

As a result of the special character of the Pauline Letters we are obliged to refer in particular to the four Gospels in dealing with most of the happenings in the life of Jesus.

If one begins by taking these Gospels as a single unity, then in the unanimous view of all the experts the Gospel according to Mark is considered the oldest. It was available to Luke and Matthew, and was used as the basis of the later Gospels. For this reason Mark, Luke and Matthew have a similar structure and contain by and large the same material, so that they have been called the Synoptic Gospels in contrast to John.

Nevertheless further reports were available to Luke and Matthew, other than the Mark Gospel. These were used to supplement the Mark material. Since numerous sayings of Jesus are to be found both in Luke and in Matthew which have not been taken out of Mark, one has rightly drawn the conclusion that both — the Mark text apart — have used a further identical text. Amongst experts this is known as the Logia (Logien-Quelle), or Q for short. The recently found 'Thomas Gospel' must in all probability be considered as a further development of this Q source. If this view is relevant, then the Logia, which can be reconstructed from the Thomas Gospel in combination with the Luke and Matthew texts, together with the Mark text, must be considered as the oldest directly or indirectly available sources concerning Jesus. These have been used in conjunction with further material from Luke and Matthew, which has now been lost. The establishment of these pieces of evidence indicates at the same time the age of these sources relative to each other.

It has not been possible to reach any mutual agreement among scholars concerning the date at which the individual texts were written down. In my opinion the joint works of Luke — the Gospel and the Acts of the Apostles — play a key role in the solution of this question. Most New Testament scholars tend to the view that the joint works were written down in about the year 80. They give the following reasons for this relatively late dating:

1. As has already been noted, the Gospel according to St. Mark was already available to the compiler. If the Gospel according to St. Mark was set down in writing in its present form

6 1 Corinth 11, 23 ff.

5

shortly before 70, as many scholars suppose, then it leads to the year 80 for Luke, as a certain length of time must be assumed between the two.

2. In Jesus' prophecy concerning the fall of Jerusalem Luke has given some details which go beyond the formulations of Mark. Many scholars hold the theory that Luke may have inserted these sentences in the Mark text on the basis of his knowledge of the actual siege and fall of Jerusalem. If this supposition is true, then Luke can only have been written after the year 70.

3. Luke is not expecting the end of the world and the coming again of Christ in the immediate future, but states repeatedly that no one knows the time and the hour. Many New Testament scholars are of the opinion that his view is contrary to the original opinions of the early Christian communities. This would indicate a later date of composition.

A closer consideration, however, indicates that none of these reasons stands up to examination, as all are based on unproven prejudices. The points are considered in the above order:

1. There is no compulsive reason why the Mark Gospel should be placed just before the fall of Jerusalem; as is now widely argued. It cannot be excluded that the Mark Gospel was already written down earlier. Some very recent decipherings of papyri could in the long run force us to accept an earlier dating. They are at the moment, however, the subject of fierce debate.

2. Among the additions which are to be found in Luke but not in Mark, there are the sentences, 'But when you see Jerusalem encircled by armies, then you may be sure that her destruction is near'[7] and 'They will fall at the sword's point; they will be carried captive into all countries; and Jerusalem will be trampled down by foreigners until their day has run its course.'[8] These sentences suit almost every capture of a Græco-Roman city. Above all, however, they do not go beyond that which is found in the apocalyptical literature of the Jews at that time. They do not presuppose that the writer had knowledge of the actual happenings at the destruction of Jerusalem.

3. There were evidently various groups of followers in early Christianity. There was apparently disagreement on the question of the timing of the coming again of Christ. In the Mark Gospel there are already indications of differing opinions. Paul especially

7 Luke 21, 20.        8 Luke 21, 24.

6

warns against certain early expectations.[9] In view of these circumstances the systematic contention that the early Christians expected the immediate coming again of Christ, and went over to an indeterminate period of waiting only after Christ's failure to appear, can only be traced to a more or less arbitrary psychological reconstruction, which cannot be deduced from the sources. Since there is, however, no compelling reason for a late dating of the Luke Gospel — and this is indicated on critical examination — then the reasons which speak for an earlier date must be examined even more critically. The Acts of the Apostles then assume a key position.

It is especially significant that in the Acts of the Apostles, there is not one single indication given of the Jewish war which was raging from 66 onwards, nor of the destruction of Jerusalem in the year 70, and that in the whole of Luke's works there is no direct or indirect indication whatsoever of the death of the apostles Peter and Paul.

The attempt which is made now and then to suggest that Paul's farewell address in Ephesus, in Chapter 20 of the Acts of the Apostles, is an indirect indication of the actual death of Paul is absolutely beside the point. The decisive sentences of this address read, 'And now, as you see, I am on my way *to Jerusalem*, under the constraint of the Spirit. Of what will befall me there I know nothing, except that in city after city the Holy Spirit assures me that imprisonment and hardships await me. For myself, I set no store on life; I only want to finish the race, and complete the task which the Lord Jesus assigned to me, of bearing my testimony to the gospel of God's grace. One word more: I have gone about among you proclaiming the Kingdom, but now I know that none of you will see my face again.'[10]

Anyone who reads these sentences impartially would never think than an indication is hereby given of the actual death of Paul *in Rome*. Why did Luke make Paul's fears refer so clearly to Jerusalem? As the first Letter to the Thessalonians bears witness, Paul made a factual prophecy to his followers of the oppressions

9  Mark 13, 7 and 13, 10 for example indicate a longer time to the 'end', whereas
   13, 20 can indicate an early expectation. Finally 13, 32 stresses that no one
   knows the day and the hour. Paul also warns against early expectations, as
   in 1. Thess 20, 1 ff.
10  Acts 20, 22 ff.

7

which lay before him.[11] The whole situation in Jerusalem was extremely tense at the time; Paul only just escaped being murdered! Finally Jerusalem was the city, according to the conviction held at that time, in which the prophets were murdered. In view of the threatening overall situation Paul wrote to the Romans, 'I implore you by our Lord Jesus Christ and by the love that the Spirit inspires, be my allies in the fight; pray to God for me that I may be saved from unbelievers *in Judaea* and that my errand to Jerusalem may find acceptance with God's people.'[12] It can be concluded from this whole evidence that the farewell address in Ephesus, which is formulated in Luke, mirrors the fears which Paul actually uttered before he went to Jerusalem. It is not possible, on the other hand, without violating the facts, to consider this address as an indication freely conceived by Luke of the death of Paul *in Rome.*

The whole style of the last chapter of the Acts of the Apostles speaks against such an interpretation. In Jerusalem a kind of low ebb is reached with the imprisonment and attempted murder. From that point onwards there follows the release, which is described detail for detail, fully in every phase, right up to the final sentence, 'He stayed ... proclaiming the kingdom of God and teaching the facts about the Lord Jesus Christ quite openly and without hindrance.'[13] Luke does not give the slightest indication of the approaching oppressions or even of Paul's approaching death.

There is one further point, and that not the least impressive, namely that in the 19th chapter of the Acts of the Apostles Paul gives Rome as his destination, after Jerusalem, 'When I have been there (Jerusalem), I must also see Rome — δεῖ με καὶ ʿΡώμην ἰδεῖν.'[14] It can be stated with certainty that Luke would never have formulated this announcement in this way *after* the death of Paul. He would not have used the verb ἰδεῖν but a more ambiguous formula such as 'give witness also in Rome' μαρτυρεῖν)'. A careful examination of all the appropriate places in the Acts of the Apostles thus shows that Luke gives no indication at all of the actual death of Paul in Rome.

Naturally an argument *ex silentio* only holds good in particular cases. One cannot draw the conclusion that certain

11  1. Thess 3, 4.      12  Romans 13, 30 f.
13  Acts 28, 31.      14  Acts 19, 21.

8

events which are not mentioned were consequently unknown to him. The following considerations force us to the conclusion that Luke in fact had no knowledge of the aforementioned events. The Jewish war is an important part of the history of the early Church. The original followers in Jerusalem lose their significance through the war. With the destruction of Jerusalem Jesus' prophecy is moreover fulfilled. If Luke had been writing after 70, it would be incomprehensible that he should break off his narrative shortly before the fulfilment of Jesus' prophecy, and not indicate the fate of the followers in Jerusalem.

It is equally unthinkable that Luke knew of the death of Peter, and especially that of Paul, without reporting the facts. The most important fact is that Paul is the central figure of the greater part of the Acts of the Apostles. Luke describes the effect of his work, and his suffering for the gospel, in great detail. For what reasons would the selfsame Luke, who described the martyrdom of Stephan so penetratingly, withhold from his readers the crowning conclusion of the Witness to Christ of the apostle Paul?

Each of these arguments carries its own weight. Moreover they support and complement each other. The question arises, 'Why should Luke, if he had only been writing in the year 80, break off his report on the early church so arbitrarily at the very point where the Acts of Apostles in fact stops?

In the search for an answer to this question it has at times been stated that, according to Luke's account, Jesus promised the apostles at his Ascension that they would bear witness to him 'all over Judea and Samaria, and away to the ends of the earth'.[15] This promise might be considered to be fulfilled with the coming of Paul to Rome. Therefore the Acts of the Apostles closes with these events.[16]

15 Acts 1, 8.

16 Gerhard Lohfink, in his book 'Jetzt verstehe ich die Bibel', says on p. 59, '. . . he (Paul) was put to death in the capital at the end of his Roman imprisonment. Luke moreover knew that, but he no longer mentions it, because he was not interested in telling the story of Paul or even the Apostles. His aim was solely to present the origin and growth of the church — as far as Rome. He could therefore close with the arrival of the great missionary Paul in Rome.' The fact that there was a Christian community in Rome before 'the arrival of the great missionary Paul' is not mentioned at all, but is indirectly played down by the above wording. The decisive question is also unanswered, as to why Luke actually denies the crowning achievement of Paul's witnesses to Christ, in that he emphasizes without

These views are not convincing, as on the one hand, Rome, the capital of the world, is nowhere described in the literature of that time as the 'end of the earth'; on the other hand, as it appears from the Acts of the Apostles, Christianity had taken hold in Rome before Paul, so that one cannot maintain that the first proclamation of Christianity in Rome was a key happening for Luke. In addition the question would naturally remain outstanding as to why the testimony of the martyrdom of the apostle *in Rome* is not worth a single word or indication.

In view of all this it can be clearly stated that Luke especially, who has a noticeable feeling for history, would certainly not have broken off the Acts of the Apostles at this point, if he had known of the death of Peter and Paul, and of the destruction of Jerusalem. It would not only have been more impressive but also more sensible to have ended the Acts of the Apostles with those happenings by means of which important themes, already treated in detail by Luke, reach a satisfactory conclusion. The available text of the Acts of the Apostles leads the impartial scholar to the conclusion that Luke finished the Acts of the Apostles even before these happenings, and sent the work to Theophilus.

As has already been mentioned, the necessity of giving an early dating to Luke has as its result the giving of an early dating to the Mark Gospel, which must then have been written down in the fifties.

There is almost unanimous agreement that Matthew, or alternatively the final composer of the Matthew Gospel, did not complete his work in its present form before the year 80.

All previous reflections on the problem have been concerned with the date of the actual writing down in its present form. Brief mention has already been made of other — sometimes older — scripts, which have been lost. Added to this is the fact that an oral fixation of large parts of the text preceded the written fixation. Even Willi Marxsen provokes the thought 'that the transition from an oral to a written tradition is in so far continuous since a relative fixation of the material in the oral tradition was almost equal to a written fixation.'[17]

any reservation that Paul 'without hindrance' proclaimed the kingdom of God and the teaching of the Lord Jesus Christ in all frankness.'
17 Marxsen, Willi, Einleitung in das Neue Testament, Gütersloh, third edition 1964, p. 113.

The Scandinavian scholar, Thorleif Boman recently had this to say concerning the acceptance in general of earlier works: 'Folklore teaches us that if a tradition arises from a historical figure, then this tradition forms an integrated story, because the person — and not the individual deed — stands in the middle of the account. A lack of knowledge about the result of research on modern folklore is indicated if Bultmann, together with Dibelius, sees the task of form-criticism as 'to reconstruct the origin and history of these fragments in order to clarify the history of pre-literary tradition'.[18]

Whether one goes as far as Boman or not, and assumes that the Jesus tradition forms 'a connected story' from the very beginning, one must admit quite independently that every serious scholarly theory, in contrast to those of Bultmann, Marxsen etc., starts from the assumption that the Jesus tradition deals from the very outset with a complete tradition. The fact that both then and now isolated sayings of Jesus, the happenings in his life, are read out in divine services or told in sermons, is not disputed. Nevertheless ... it is not a matter of considering individual passages, even if a firm order and sequence is missing. The interest of those who narrated and heard the sayings and stories of Jesus is not concerned with the brilliant episode or the marvellous expression of a single saying, but with Jesus the Person, through whose deeds, death, and resurrection the prophecies of the Old Testament had been fulfilled. The cohesion of the tradition was thus ensured through Jesus the Person, and through the interest of the relevant narrator and listener in this person.

The unity of the early Jesus tradition does not therefore depend on the arrangement of the material in the same sort of way as it would in a reminiscence about a particularly impressive personality. If people not only tell anecdotes of some kind or other in order to pass the time, but also turn with a certain seriousness to a particular person, as for example when children speak of their dead father, or when pupils speak of a former teacher, or members of a congregation of a former priest or minister, then the arrangement of the material is certainly not chronological or systematic, but more or less determined by

18 Bomann, Thorleif, Die Jesus-Überlieferung im Lichte der neueren Volkskunde, Göttingen 1967, p. 35.

11

association. Yet all that which is told forms a unity of a certain kind.

Thorleif Boman assumes in general that the material for a narrative is already brought into a firm sequence in the oral tradition, and writes, 'The structure of the Mark Gospel, thought out carefully for its mnemonic use in the memory, cannot be based on chance. It must therefore have been worked out for oral delivery, also in the form in which we know it.'[19]

This proposition has much to be said for it, especially if one does not connect it with the supposition 'that the Mark Gospel was fundamentally an official account of the public deeds of Jesus, which the earliest Christians and the original apostles caused to be worked out for future use,'[20] but if one leaves this question open.

It is abundantly clear from the fact itself, and it is almost indisputable, that the story of the Crucifixion has been handed down from the beginning as a complete story. Perhaps, as Boman suggests, the remaining material was put into a firm sequence by certain prophets, for the first time, on the occasion of the oral transmission. In this way, judging from the matter itself, there were certain sections which fitted into a certain place in the sequence, such as the baptism of Jesus by John, and the accounts of His suffering and death. The arrangement of the remaining material was subject to a certain arbitrary choice. From general experience with similar traditions it can be assumed that the sequence of actual events was kept, in so far as the remembrance of them was still vivid, though in many cases there were no such recollections. The experiences which we enjoy today can be used in our own recollections. For example, if someone should write down, without notes, his recollections of his father or of a teacher, then there would be certain fixed points in the chronology which he could remember with certainty. He would more or less have to fit in the remaining material at his own discretion.

'Source Q', from which Luke and Matthew took many of Jesus' sayings, and which, as has been previously mentioned, probably has the Thomas Gospel as its basis, is a special manifestation. The Thomas Gospel, which is apparently related to 'Source Q' in structure, if considered according to its literary classification, is not a gospel.

It does not contain a report of the passion, death and

19 op. cit. p. 95.     20 op. cit. p. 47.

12

resurrection, but consists of 114 sayings of Jesus, which are arranged in a loose order, and are generally introduced with the words 'Jesus said'. This peculiarity can be most convincingly explained if one relates it to the prevailing times, and the fact that in Jesus' time the Rabbi students collected and learnt by heart the sayings and teachings of their respective masters. It is highly probable that the disciples of Jesus behaved in a similar way before the great crisis. That would mean to say that the matrix of a collection of Jesus' sayings was already fixed before his passion and death. Should this theme be right, then it is conceivable that 'source Q' was over a long period only fixed orally, and that sections of this oral tradition were carried over into the gospels. This would at the same time be an adequate explanation for the fact that there is a different arrangement of the individual sayings in Luke, Matthew, and in the Thomas Gospel.

Apart from the Mark Gospel and 'Source Q', further sources were available to the writers of the Luke and Matthew Gospels. In the course of setting down their Gospels they had to carry out a certain editing, just as the editor of a book who makes use of a number of sources is forced to do. In particular they had to decide how they could link the individual pieces of material with each other, also which sections they should follow in cases of variance, and which pieces of their own material they would have to leave out.

In contrast to many modern editors they were very careful to preserve the traditional material. With what detailed care they managed to avoid strong changes is shown, for example, in several places in the Matthew Gospel. A number of the sayings of Jesus appear in two different places, because Matthew apparently found them in two different sources, each in a different context. In chapter 18, there is a point which is taken over from Mark, reading, 'If your hand or your foot is your undoing, cut it off and fling it away; it is better for you to enter into life maimed or lame, than to keep two hands or two feet and be thrown into the eternal fire. If it is your eye that is your undoing, tear it out and fling it away; it is better to enter into life with one eye than to keep both eyes and be thrown into the fires of hell'. The same saying is to be found in chapter 5. Here it says, 'If your right eye leads you astray, tear it out and fling it away; it is better for you to lose one part of your body than for the whole of it to be thrown into hell.

And if your right hand is your undoing, cut it off and fling it away; it is better for you to lose one part of your body than for the whole of it to go to hell.'

A comparison of these two quotations incidentally shows the questionable way in which Rudolf Bultmann conducts a scholarly argument. He writes, 'The same unconscious need for a specific vividness appears here, just as in the relationship of Matthew 5, 29.30 to Mark 9, 43, 45, 47; whilst in Mark there is in general only talk of hand, foot, and eye, in Matthew the right eye and the right hand are named.'[21] Bultmann fails to reveal that Matthew, in the passage taken over from Mark, namely 18, 8 ff, just like Mark speaks 9, 43 ff only of hand, foot, and eye, and that on the other hand the Matthew passage 5, 29 f in which the talk is of the right eye and the right hand, is not taken from Mark at all, but apparently from another source, the age of which we are not able to ascertain in relation to Mark.

Such passages which are often called doubles — and of which there are a number — show that it was far from the intent of the compiler of the Matthew Gospel to carry out his editing task with a certain self-willed sovereignty. He was more concerned to bring together into a single work that which he found in the various sources.

The same applies to Luke. As Marxsen rightly remarks, the introduction to the Gospel shows that it was his intention to replace the former records with an especially careful and complete account.[22] In fact, with the exception of the Mark text, which was already widely distributed and was perhaps the official one, all pre-Luke gospels have been lost, although there were probably more of them than most of the modern commentators assume. It can also be noticed in profane history that older accounts are quickly lost when better and more complete works are published. The fate of most of Livy's predecessors need only be mentioned in this respect. There is no valid reason for attempting to explain away the introductory remark of Luke's, according to which, 'many have undertaken the drawing up of an account of the events which have taken place among us . . .'[23] In

21 Bultmann, Rudolf, Die Geschichte der synoptischen Tradition, Göttingen, sixth edition 1964, p. 340.
22 Marxsen, Willi, Der Streit um die Bibel, Gladbeck 1965, p. 83.
23 Luke 1, 1.

my opinion the variations of the Luke text from the Mark text, which Luke follows in the essentials, can be traced not only to his own editorial work, but also go back to older sources to which Luke gave preference in the relevant places. In that respect the theological intentions of Luke lie less in a fully individualistic transformation of the text than in the relevant decision between two different prototypes.

The origin of the John gospel is still relatively unexplained in spite of numerous attempts. Not so long ago there was the tendency to consider the Gospel according to St. John as having a Hellenistic imprint, and assign to it practically no value as a historical source.

Nevertheless one continues to wonder at the fact that the chronological and even the geographical details in John are more convincing in many places than in the Synoptic Gospels, and one ascertains with surprise that the details of places mentioned in the John gospel have been confirmed in many cases by excavations. In the last few decades moreover, it has been proved that many expressions in the John gospel, which one formerly assumed to be Hellenistic, are in fact Jewish-Essenic.

In view of this whole situation many experts nowadays assume that the John Gospel goes back to good old traditions, and that in spite of its relatively late fixing in its final written form, it is in many respects perhaps the very earliest gospel, 'whose tradition was formed in Jerusalem before the destruction. That does not mean to say that the book in its present form did not have a long literary development behind it; but it contains old historical traditions, which found their shape in Aramaic or Hebrew-speaking surroundings, where the Essenic way of thinking was still very much alive.[24]

It is not possible in this brief investigation to go into the difficult problem of the John Gospel in detail. It can at least be said with certainty that the John Gospel was fixed in writing in the first century, and contains significantly more genuine tradition than one first assumed.[25] The establishment of this fact is

24 Cross, Frank Moore, Die antike Bibliothek von Qumrab, Neukirchen 1967, p. 194 f.

25 This dating has been verified by a papyrus fragment which is now in the possession of the John Rylands Library in Manchester. This may well be given a date at the end of the first or the beginning of the second century. (cf. Eric Stier, op. cit., on this point).

15

especially important for historical research, because the compiler of the John Gospel bears no literary dependence on the Synoptics, but 'must always be seen as an independent source, as an original witness of the first tradition.'[26]

26 Jerusalem Bibel, Freiburg 1968, p. 1492.

# 3. The reliability of the gospels as historical sources

## (a) General considerations

When one considers that the fixation of the reports on the life and work of Jesus began at an early date, then it is astounding, that considerable differences are to be found between each of the Gospels. A large part of these divergences can of course be understood in the sense of being supplementary material. The Logia, for example, must have preserved many of the sayings of Jesus which are not reported in the Mark Gospel. The same can be said of the special sources in Matthew, Luke, and also John.

In spite of all these differences the Gospels as a whole present an essentially harmonious and complete picture of Jesus. This fact is at times neglected, in view of the research into detail which is so prevalent today. Yet notice should certainly be taken of the fact that a person who reads the Gospels one after the other gets the impression that here are texts which agree the one with the other. It is very rarely that it is immediately noticeable that this or that detail is presented in a different way.

Only a person who has become aware of this fact, and then begins to study comparatively, notices that besides the passages which help to complete the tradition there are also anomalies which could well be considered as contradictions. The one kind of narration automatically excludes the other. Here are two examples to prove this point.

1. According to the accounts given in Mark and Luke Jesus is staying in Peter's house, and then heals a leper. In the account given by Matthew the healing of the leper takes place first, and then follows the stay in Peter's house.'[27]

27 cf. Mark 1, 29–45, and Luke 4, 38 f.; Luke 5, 12 ff. with Matt 8, 1–4 and 14 f.
   Such differences show in addition how one-sided the view is that variations of the Matthew (and also the Luke) text from the Mark text have to be traced back in every case to theological intentions. Whereas in previous

17

2. In Matthew the centurion of Capernaum himself talks with Jesus, whereas in Luke he sends 'some Jewish elders' and friends, who convey his request.'[28]

Quite apart from the attitude which one may otherwise take towards the question of miracles, one must draw the conclusion from the examples given that the Gospels do not give accounts which are historically accurate in every detail.

The historian knows, however, that in the whole of profane literature — such as in memoirs — such variations do occur. These even occur in sources which one generally considers reliable. Nobody took down notes on the spot, or recorded accurately all the incidents regarding when and where Jesus stayed, and what he did and said. Even if the first oral fixations already occurred only a few years after the death of Jesus, the time lapse causes a certain unreliability or rather imprecision in the sources on matters of detail.

Experience of profane history teaches us especially that in all those places where the chronology does not forcibly arise as the result of definite actions, or of the concurrence of events which have easily remembered fixed points in the calendar, such as public holidays, then a certain vagueness very soon sets in, as to when and in what order the events took place. The same applies to place names, in so far as the places concerned are not themselves irrevocably tied up with the sequence of events. Of course, the same applies also to other statements on matters of detail.

The historian must fundamentally reckon with the same weaknesses of the memory, and the same irritating flights of fancy, as the lawyer. The experience of every investigating authority goes to show that even in cases where the witnesses are ordered to report only that which they can remember with certainty, yet differences occur between the testimonies of the witnesses, even between the testimonies given in good faith by such witnesses. The statements made by the witnesses to a traffic accident provide a good example.

---

periods the theological intentions of the actual compilers were given too little attention, many modern exegetists are nowadays inclined to go to the other extreme.

28 cf. Matt 8, 5 ff. with Luke 7, 1 ff.

The historian therefore reckons as a matter of course with those anomalies and imprecisions in the writings of the New Testament which are found in comparable sources in profane literature. Three points are worth noting.
1. Details of time and place are not to be considered reliable unless they are directly connected with decisive events. For this reason the naming of the place 'in the Jordan' at Jesus' baptism, the naming of the exact location 'in the place of his birth' during a certain controversy over Jesus, and the name 'Jerusalem' during Jesus' lamentations, all these are of greater historical significance than place names on the occasion of some miracle or other, or connected with parables. The same applies to details of time. It can be said with greater certainty that the arrest, the sufferings of Christ on the cross, and the death of Jesus occurred about the time of the Feast of the Passover, and that this general assertion is more accurate, apart from any questions of detail, than to make such statements as 'on the following day', and similar ones, where happenings are described which could just as well have taken place on another day.

In view of the fact that most of the events which are recorded in the Gospels need not in themselves be related to a definite place or date, but could equally well have taken place here or there, or alternatively earlier or later, there results a certain arbitrariness in the sequence and in the compilation. One also has to reckon with the possibility that the sayings of Jesus were combined with certain events and other matters at a later date.

In any assessment of the speeches and sermons which are recorded in the Gospels and the Acts of the Apostles, the tradition behind the classical way of writing history must be taken into consideration. From a historical point of view it is an artificially created problem if modern commentators discover with apparent surprise that in a comparison of the speeches of Jesus in the Synoptic Gospels and those in the Gospel according to St. John there is a variation in style. Erich Stier had this to say during a symposium of the Deutsches Institut für Bildung und Wissen in 1969, 'The critical onlooker of the four canonical Gospels can be led through a superficial study of the problem to the conclusion that the harmonious handing down which is seen in the three Synoptic Gospels makes the speeches of Jesus, as recorded in the John Gospel, appear to be 'not genuine'. This conclusion is seen to be premature as soon as one starts to compare it with one of the most reliable heathen historical sources, namely that which was compiled by the Athenian Thucydides, and which is noted for its astounding objectivity, especially on the history of the Peleponesian War. It can be said with certainty that the magnificent passage in that work, namely the dying speech of Pericles, cannot have been held by that famous statesman in its present form. The experts are nevertheless in no doubt that it is based on authentic material, and must be considered a valid document concerning the intellectual attitude and manner of thinking of Pericles. It is evident that criteria which could be worked out over generations for the objective assessment of an original work, namely a tried and critical form of research achieved by almost unbroken labour, that all this also demands respect outside the bounds of specialized history. What is right for the works of Thucydides is also reasonable for the Gospel according to St. John as a historical document. Any other procedure would be irresponsible, seen from the point of view of modern historical scholarship.'[29]

Certain deviations from the actual happenings can only cause surprise in someone who has never concerned himself intensively with historical sources. A historically accurate recording of all the dates, places, and events only takes place where a record is continuously kept. This is, however, not the case with most historical sources. Let us suppose, for example, that one goes to the trouble for once of studying the details of the reports on the battle in the Teutoburger Wald or on the fire in the Reichstag in 1933. It is only after this sort of experience that one can form an opinion about the historical credibility of the Gospels, for one must apply the same criteria in both cases, assuming that the use of other criteria cannot be scientifically justified.

2. It must be expected that the different versions of the Gospels present one-sided interpretations of what Jesus did and what Jesus said. A part of the difference between the Gospels can obviously be traced back to that fact. In literature it has been pointed out for a long time now that the manner of presentation depends on the recipients at whom the writings are aimed. Thus it may be said that the Matthew Gospel was primarily prepared

29 In 'Moderne Exegese und historische Wissenschaft' op. cit. p. 56 f.

20

for Jewish Christians, whereas Luke addressed himself above all to the heathen Christian reader.

Anyone who reads the Gospels attentively can confirm the accuracy of such statements. They are not enough, though, to explain the differences already mentioned. A further matter must be taken into account, which is, that there were all sorts of people who joined Jesus and became his followers: men who were originally strict Thora-Jews, and some who were close to the sects of the Essenes, and finally members of groups who aimed at social reforms. They all listened to Jesus. Yet how they understood him depended very much on their way of thinking before they met Him.

In this way the particular disciples did not interpret the sayings of Jesus first in retrospect and according to their prior understanding, but they understood Him each according to his own general attitude, which was right from the very start oriented in the one or the other direction. This is certainly credible when the Gospels repeatedly state that at first even the closest of Jesus' followers seriously misunderstood Him, and only corrected their false expectations after the crucifixion and the resurrection of Jesus. In spite of everything the individual characteristics of the first witnesses continue to be effective in the Gospel texts. The historian finds that such ways of interpreting events, which are partly one-sided, as something which is quite natural. In our political everyday life speeches are also occasionally so reported and interpreted in different ways in the newspapers so that the impression arises that only one of the reports can be correct. Only a comparison of the actual words used in the speech tends to reveal that none of the newspapers has actually reported anything false.

Such an example would arise, if a politician in a speech stressed on the one hand his love of peace, and yet mentions the determination with which one is prepared to defend oneself if the occasion arises. Thus one reporter can underline the expressions concerning the love of peace, whilst another stresses the determination to defend.

The variations are as a rule the greater, the more the reporter is personally involved. The person who is inwardly involved tends to stress those things which touch him personally — as he thinks — expressing them still more clearly and better

21

than they were actually spoken, yet on the other hand subconsciously missing hearing, or deliberately omitting or toning down other matters. In doing that he only has the feeling that he is handing on even more clearly and distinctly that which he is reporting. This is not a matter of deliberate falsification but of intended clarification, which — as the reporter believes — represents the important points correctly and especially well.

The fact that the sayings of Jesus were seen both then and now as a guide to one's own decisions is not the least of the considerations. We must accordingly reckon that the sayings of Jesus which have been handed down were accentuated to meet the acute questionings of the early followers, or were also supplemented by amplifications, by way of interpretation.

3. When once a person has moved into the central position of a tradition, and especially when extraordinary achievements are reported, then an extension and a supplementing of the accounts of his deeds quickly follow. On the one hand supplements which are historically genuine are taken in hand, in that the whole of the tradition — as far as it is still accessible in an oral or written form — is carefully collected: on the other hand supplementary material and embellishments follow, which are figments of the imagination and do not represent the facts.

A difference must be drawn between the embellishment of facts, which basically belong to the genuine tradition, and the acceptance of deeds and sayings which were originally reported by other people. In many cases such embellishments and traditions can clearly be shown to be non-historical. Of course it often cannot be cleared up, whether a supplementing of the material is a spontaneous embellishment or a complementary account from good old traditions. There is another factor in dealing with parallel accounts, namely whether a certain theme is transferred from a central figure to another person, or whether in fact similar happenings occurred to the one and the other person. The descriptions of life in the Middle Ages offer a rich source of material for the problems concerned.

For all the reasons given, which could be further developed, it is not possible in many cases to clarify, from the detailed statements given in a historical account, whether this or that took place exactly in the way described. This applies also to the Gospels. It can often be said with a good degree of probability,

22

sometimes with certainty, that some detail or other has been twisted, embellished, or otherwise changed in relation to the original occurrence. All this, however, does not take away the credibility of a historical document as a whole. There is widespread unanimity on this point.

## (b) *The history of Jesus and the preaching of the Gospel*

The greatest objection to the value of the Gospels as source material does not arise nowadays from considerations such as have just been described, but arises from a fundamental question, which is that in modern theological literature we are not concerned in the Gospels with historical description but with the preaching of the Gospel. The concern is not the narration of certain facts, but a message of salvation to mankind. A theologian such as Rudolf Bultmann assures us, 'The Christ who is proclaimed is not the historical Jesus but the Christ of Faith and of Worship'.[30] Marxsen, referring to Bornkamm, writes with a different accentuation, but still rejecting a historical interpretation of the Gospels, 'The original disciples were not concerned to describe who Jesus was, but who he is'.[31]

Supposing that the Evangelists did not, in fact, wish to give a historical description, then a considerable encroachment on the validity of the Gospels results, in the sense of them making up a historical document, an encroachment which goes far beyond anything which has previously been said on the subject.

In actual fact there can be no doubt that the Evangelists are not reporting narrative history for the sake of narrative history; that they did not want to write (as Marxsen phrases it) a 'history text-book'[32]; and that they were primarily concerned with a message of salvation.

On the other side of the fence the historian must well question whether the alternative put forward by Bultmann, Marxsen, and others really serves any useful purpose in solving the question. The historian feels himself obliged to call attention to the following practical points and facts.

1. It is not everyone who practises history who does so for

30  Bultmann, op. cit. p. 396.
31  Marxsen, op. cit. Introduction p. 114 f.
32  Marxsen, op. cit. The Dispute p. 22.

the sake of history itself. Numerous great works in history came about in order to bring out the then prevailing lustre of a certain dynastic family, in order to give substance to the prevailing claims and rights, or to establish and maintain the prevailing political circumstances or decisions. As Hans-Georg Gadamer convincingly demonstrates in his standard work 'Wahrheit und Methode'[33] (Truth and Method), such a contemporary interest is a legitimate attitude in one who pursues history. It is very much open to question whether there would ever have been historical scholarship without this impulse.

2. Anyone who is interested in another person because he wants to enter into close ties, or wants to make friends, or to cooperate professionally with him enquires first what this particular person has done up to date. A curriculum vitae, a personal record, without any gaps, is demanded of every person who applies for a leading position in life. If two people strike up a friendship, it sometimes happens that the one or the other spontaneously says, 'You don't really know who I am.' Then he begins to give an account of an episode out of his previous life. In that well-known reference book 'Who is Who' the details which predominate are those concerned with the previous life of the individual. From all this it can be seen that he who wants to know who a person is, enquires who a person was.

The above considerations show how misleading the alternative theme is, 'The original disciples were not concerned to describe who Jesus was, but who Jesus is', because the fact that one asks who somebody was, in order to find out who he is, is really part of a person's everyday experience. Not the opposite.

Of course the objection could be raised that with Jesus we are dealing with a very special case, since the accounts of His work and His suffering were only gathered and drafted after the experience of the resurrection. Without a shadow of a doubt it has to be granted that experience of the actual resurrection does not belong to a person's normal, everyday experience, and therefore cannot be compared, without further explanation, with other experiences.

On the other hand the general situation which is spoken of here comes up frequently. Anyone who writes about a historical personality conceives of his whole account with the impression of

33 Gadamer, Hans George, Wahrheit und Methode, Tübingen 1965.

especially outstanding and fateful events clearly in mind. For example, anyone who is writing about Hitler deals with the years leading up to the seizure of power, and the years of the phoney peace in the Third Reich, with the frightful catastrophe of the Second World War and the cumulation of the inhuman terror within Germany in mind. Such a concept by no means leads forcibly to a false picture of history. On the contrary. Since the author concerned knows the final culmination in all its naked brutality, he is in a better position to understand the numerous actions and utterances of Hitler than they were understood at a time when doubt and illusions could still exist about the whole concept of National Socialism, and when one did not know with absolute certainty whether certain manifestations were abuses or fundamental elements of the system.

The individual undergoes similar experiences in his daily life. How often does someone say after a particular event, 'Now I see why Mother did this, or said that, at that particular time'. It can be a shaking experience when the relatives realize after the death of a person that they did not take notice of, or seriously misunderstood certain utterances and actions of the dead person. Then one is prepared to say, 'He knew very well that it would not last long, and therefore wanted to put everything right'. The same basic narrative structure can be seen here, namely that certain actions and words of a person are fully understood in retrospect, under the impression of subsequent events. When the Evangelists repeatedly report that the disciples had not understood this or that saying of Jesus *at the time* (i.e. before the crucifixion and the resurrection), but nevertheless remembered the fact later, then this process represents our everyday experience exactly.

It can therefore be generally stated that it is beyond question that the Gospels were first drawn up after the resurrection, and under the impression left by the resurrection. That does not mean in any way that the prior historical incidents have necessarily been falsely reported. On the contrary. It is equally possible that they were able to see and to judge the prior historical incidents correctly for the first time for this very reason.

If the question were to be asked, in view of these preliminary reflections, how the writers of the New Testament themselves saw the relationship between the preaching of the Gospel and the historical facts then the answer is clear: according to their convictions, the preaching of the Gospel by Jesus irrevocably includes the testimony of historical events.

In the 15th chapter of the Apostle Paul's First Letter to the Corinthians are these words, 'First and foremost I handed on to you the facts which have been imparted to me: that Christ died for our sins, in accordance with the scriptures; and that he appeared to Cephas, and afterwards to the Twelve. Then he appeared to over five hundred of our brothers at once, most of whom are still alive, though some have died. Then he appeared to James, and afterwards to all the apostles. In the end he appeared even to me; though this birth of mine was monstrous.'[34] Paul is trying here to provide the evidence of witnesses by naming people who can be unmistakenly identified, and who can bear witness to a definite event, namely the appearance of Jesus after his death.

Only if the first apostles did in fact consider it important to give witness to certain events historically, is it comprehensible that, according to the account handed down in the Acts of the Apostles, Peter does not allow just any devout and eloquent man to be chosen as an Apostle in the place of the fallen Judas, but he clearly limits the circle of possible candidates, in that he declares, 'Therefore one of those who bore us company all the while we had the Lord Jesus with us, coming and going, from John's ministry of baptism until the day when he was taken up from us — one of those must now join us as a witness to his resurrection.'[35] Also this incident shows that certain events had to be attested. For a simple proclamation of the Gospel, not depending on the historical facts, an eyewitness who had been present during the whole of Jesus' public appearances, beginning with the baptism by John, would not have been necessary.

The exact wording of the sermon given at Pentecost can be referred to in the same connection. Peter firstly refers the Jews to that of which they themselves have been witness, when he says, 'I speak of Jesus of Nazareth, a man singled out by God and made known to you through miracles, portents, and signs, which God worked among you through him, *as you well know*. When he had been given up to you, by the deliberate will and plan of God, you used heathen men to crucify and kill him.'[36] He then adds in a

34 1. Corinth 15, 3–8.     35 Acts 1, 21 f.     36 Acts 2, 22 f.

26

later passage, 'The Jesus we speak of has been raised by God, *as we can all bear witness.*'[37] In this sermon, events which the Jews know of their own accord are supplemented by others, which are testified to by the Apostles.

Specific and emphatic allusions to a personal witnessing are to be found not only at the time of the resurrection, but also in other parts of the Gospel. Thus John has this to say, 'so they did not break his legs. But one of the soldiers stabbed his side with a lance, and at once there was a flow of blood and water. This is vouched for by an eyewitness, whose evidence is to be trusted.'[38] Similarly there is the passage in the postscript at the end of John's Gospel, 'It is this same disciple who attests what has here been written. It is in fact he who wrote it, and we know that his testimony is true.'[39] Such passages show that the Evangelists are concerned with a message of salvation, but that the credibility of this message of salvation is nevertheless dependent on the credibility of definite historical facts. So the alternative question, whether the Gospels are concerned with the message of salvation, *or* with the witness to historical events, is not only falsely posed, but nonsense. Anyone who attempts to answer this question, which is falsely posed from the start, can only arrive at nonsensical answers. The Gospel show that the intention of the authors is concerned with a message of salvation — modern theology is certainly right on that point — they also show just as clearly that this message is intrinsically — that means indissolubly — tied up with the testimony to definite events, especially the death and resurrection of Jesus.

As the writings of the New Testament show, the early prophets were fully aware of this indissoluble connection. Paul writes in this sense at the end of the passage already quoted from I. Corinthians, 'If there be no resurrection, then Christ was not raised; and if Christ was not raised, then our gospel is null and void, and so is your faith; and we turn out to be lying witnesses for God, because we bore witness that he raised Christ to life, whereas, if the dead are not raised, he did not raise him.'[40] The connection between the message of salvation and the authentic testimony to certain facts cannot be stressed more unequivocally.

37 Acts 2, 32.      38 John 19, 33.
39 John 21, 24.     40 1. Corinth 15, 14 f.

27

## (c)  The 'historical' argumentation of Willi Marxsen. An excursus

In the light of the above findings it is worth while comparing these with what Willi Marxsen writes in his work 'Der Streit um die Bibel' ('The Dispute about the Bible') under the title 'Die Bibel — kein historisches Lehrbuch' ('The Bible is not a History Textbook').[41] The fact that the Bible is not a history textbook is just a platitude. I do not know anybody who does describe the Bible as a 'history textbook'. Marxsen writes, 'One should not set up one's opponent in a discussion in the way one wants him so as to be able to refute him the more easily.'[42] Yet Marxsen does precisely that of which he complains.

The whole chapter is a classic example of a pseudo-argumentation which claims to be scientific and theological. The first part of the sub-title on page 23 of his book 'The Dispute with the Science of History' taken together with a number of other expressions such as 'when historical research states . . .'[43] and 'modern historians are talking here . . .'[44] insinuate that Marxsen is coming forward in the name of, or at least as the advocate for, historical learning. The necessary specialist qualifications are missing in his case, as his performance shows.

Naturally one can no more expect from a theologian that he should be a historian at the same time, than vice versa. But every scholar should respect the territory and the approach of other scholars. A theologian should therefore not claim to be arguing as a historian if in reality he is putting forward theological ideas. Historical scholarship has its own methods and principles which must be respected by everyone who wishes to argue from a historical point of view.

One example of the way in which Marxsen argues 'historically' is shown in this one long passage, 'In Mark (and similarly in Matthew) we find the following sequence: coming of the Baptist (Mark 1, 4–8), baptism of Jesus (1, 9–11), the temptation of Jesus (1, 12–13), the arrest of John and the coming into Galilee of Jesus (1, 14), and only much later is the fact repeated in connection with the death of John the Baptist that his arrest took place at the

41 Marxsen, op. cit. The Dispute p. 22.    42 id. p. 77.
43 op. cit. p. 22.                          44 op. cit. p. 24.

instance of Herod (6, 14–29). This is a clear and lucid presentation of the sequence of events.

It is quite different in Luke. There we find the sequence: coming of John the Baptist (3, 1–18), arrest of the Baptist by Herod (3, 19–20), the baptism of Jesus (3, 21–22), the temptation of Jesus (4, 1–13), public appearance of Jesus (4, 14). This sequence is by no means clear and lucid. Here the Baptist is arrested before the baptism of Jesus, which is certainly not easily conceivable from a historical point of view. One must therefore conclude that one cannot begin to do much with these details from Luke *historically*. The events cannot have taken place in the way that Luke presents them.

Instead the Evangelist has brought out theological thinking very strongly, which he, as the only evangelist in this form, expresses (16, 16) thus, 'Until John, it was the Law and the prophets: since then, there is the good news of the kingdom of God'. This thought guides Luke in his account . . . And in order to be able to express this theological thought, which he alone notes, the Evangelist takes the historical absurdity into account that Jesus was actually baptized only after the arrest of John the Baptist. He was apparently not concerned with historical accuracy.'[45]

This summarizing statement by Marxsen is seen to be completely arbitrary, if one turns to the appropriate passages in Luke. Luke reports, 'during the high-priesthood of Annas and Caiaphas, the word of God came to John son of Zechariah in the wilderness. And he went all over the Jordan valley proclaiming a baptism in token of repentance for the forgiveness of sins . . . But Prince Herod, when he was rebuked by him over the affair of his brother's wife Herodias and for his other misdeeds, crowned them all by shutting John up in prison.'[46] Immediately following this passage there is the sentence, 'During a general baptism of the people, when Jesus too had been baptized and was praying, heaven opened and the Holy Spirit descended on him in bodily form like a dove and there came a voice from heaven, 'Thou art my Son, my Beloved; on thee my favour rests.'[47]

No unprejudiced reader could gather from this text that 'Jesus was baptized after the arrest of John the Baptist'.

45 op. cit. p. 34 f.      46 Luke 3, 2 ff.      47 Luke 3, 21 ff.

Besides, every historian knows that there are several possible ways of arranging the material in a historical account. The two most important are the chronological and thematic ones. In most descriptions of history there is a combination of both arrangements and principles. The more firmly the material is arranged thematically, the more often is it necessary to start afresh from the point of view of time. Thus, for example, in an account in which there is primarily talk of the wars which Rome was waging against the Etruscans, the Samnites, and the Gauls, there is this sentence, 'During all these wars Rome suffered internal tensions . . .'[48] Since the writer introduces the new theme, namely the internal situation, with a retrospective time reference 'during all these wars', he indicates at this point that he has interrupted the chronological sequence, and that the happenings which are reported in the following account did not take place after the aforementioned wars, but at the same period of time.

Luke does the very same thing in the passage already mentioned. As Marxsen quite rightly observes, he arranges his material much more firmly according to themes than Mark does. For that reason he is not able, in contrast to Mark, to begin the report of the baptism of Jesus with the phrase 'in those days' but is forced into a time reference which appertains to the previous text, namely ἐν τῷ βαπτισθῆναι ἅπαντα τὸν λαόν or 'Now when all the people were baptized'.[49]

So Luke uses a method of presentation which is usual and legitimate in history. After a thematic treatment of a series of events he interrupts the chronological sequence by a reference back in time, and begins with another thematic sequence of events. This method of presentation has nothing to do with a renunciation of historical accuracy.

Marxsen's wrong interpretation has such serious consequences because he is not concerned with the question whether chronological inaccuracies are found here and there in the gospels — a point which no one disputes — but because he wants to make it plausible by means of his own argumentation that Luke himself did not apparently place much value on historical

---

48 Hilgenberg, H., and others, Unsere Geschichte — unsere Welt, Vol. I, München, Second Edition 1967, p. 103.
49 Luke 3, 21. Quoted from the Authorized Version.

accuracy,[50] so that it is nonsense in the Gospel according to St. Luke to ask after the historical facts.

For that reason Marxsen interprets the beginning of the Luke gospel radically differently, in that he says in the following long quotation, 'Now, one will naturally ask how then the beginning of the Luke gospel is to be understood. The Evangelist writes amongst other matters that he has gone over the whole course of these events in detail (1, 2). One usually concludes from this that Luke is concerned with especial, historical accuracy and that one can certainly rely on his details, especially from the historical point of view. Is it then conceivable that this very evangelist has presented John the Baptist with such historical carelessness and in such a way that everyone (also he who understands nothing about historical research) is forced to say that the statement by Mark deserves priority, historically considered, over that by Luke? This question is all the more important as Luke knew the Mark gospel, as can be shown. This point will be considered later. Then Luke has handed down an account — and there cannot be the least doubt about that — which is historically inferior to its model. How can he say, then, that he has gone over the course of events in detail?

The last verse of the Luke preface (1, 4) supplies the answer which one very often does not include in one's reading, or one overlooks. It says there that Theophilus, to whom Luke dedicates his work, is to be given authentic knowledge about the matters on which he had been informed. In this particular verse Luke states the purpose of his writings. Then one can and should take him here at his word. He is writing to strengthen Theophilus in his faith. That is his declared aim. The 'exact account' is, though, subordinated to this aim, will serve it, and should let this aim become obvious. Luke is not a secular historian, who carries out historical research and who is of the opinion that he might convince Theophilus by means of historical research of the certainty of his faith, but Luke is a believer from among the original disciples. He knows that redemption was gained in the past, and that he must present the past so as to demonstrate the salvation in it. But the past must now really be presented as a 'salvation' past. He presents the past in such a way that it can show

50 Marxsen, op. cit. The Dispute p. 35.

'the certainty of faith', as it accords with the Faith, and not just in a secular manner.

That this interpretation of Luke 1, 1–4 is the correct one, has been shown to us by our consideration of the course of the story of John the Baptist. It coincides exactly with that which Luke had planned in his preface, and in the way in which we have explained the plan. If on the other hand our explanation of Luke 1, 1–4 had been false, and if one said that for Luke it were a genuine representation of history, then one would have to say in judgement that he had set himself a clear aim but he had not reached it. Since Luke was not concerned though with history, but with faith, we do not need to be surprised that he did not achieve, as we have seen, a historically accurate presentation.'[51]

The critical reader notices at once that Marxsen at this point builds his opponent up as he would like to have him. What is the purpose of such a trite statement as the point that Luke is not a secular historian, or that it was not a matter for him of 'a genuine presentation of history'? Prejudiced nonsense of this kind has not previously been stated by anybody. When one reads the above paragraphs by Marxsen one is forced to suppose that he is here building up a 'real historical' caricature in order to distract the attention of his readers, and in the meantime bringing home his own one-sided theses without attracting attention.

As a non-theologian I cannot and will not pass judgement as to whether Luke changed the more chronological sequence of Mark in favour of his own more thematic sequence for theological reasons. Since Marxsen as a theologian is of this opinion then I am prepared to agree with him. As I have explained, Luke did not undertake the alteration from Mark without regard to the historical course of events. His thematic presentation is just as correct according to the historical sequence as the chronological presentation in Mark. The statement by Marxsen that there can 'now be no further doubt' that Luke's account 'is historically inferior to its model' is therefore groundless. Thereby the main props of his otherwise very arbitrary interpretation of the first verses of Luke collapse.

Similar proof that the evangelists do not make theological statements without regard to the historical events could also be brought forward for the dating of the death of Jesus, which is

51 id. p. 36.

stated by Marxsen as a second example of a purely theological statement, whose transmitter has 'absolutely no historical interest in the date'.[52] In this brief enquiry I must be satisfied though by means of the one example to demonstrate the untenability of Marxsen's artificially exaggerated alternative, which is 'correct historically or theologically'. Evidence of this seems to me to be all the more necessary as Marxsen draws conclusions in the following paragraph from a false point of departure, which then includes yet another learned short circuit. Marxsen writes, 'Now many a person may say that the examples which have already been given are quite by the way; we have not yet approached the really central problems. Is it then permissible already now to draw such fundamental conclusions? I think the answer is 'yes'![53]

Even if Marxsen were right that the Evangelists made theological statements in the form of historical details without regard to the actual events, in passages which 'are quite by the way', such an inference would be risky; one has to accept — as the points discussed up to date have shown — that the Evangelists did not in fact, write their reports without regard to the historical events, and that the attestation of historical happenings belong indissolubly to the preaching of the Gospel. Marxsen's statement thus becomes completely untenable.

A further point. Every historian knows that sources which are concerned with 'central' happenings are generally more reliable than the description of things which are 'completely by the way'. If, for example, the numbers of bishops and princes present at a coronation are estimated differently by various sources, no historian would dream of drawing the conclusion from this that the sources are unreliable and that the coronation itself did not actually take place. The same applies to the hearing of witnesses in courts of justice. In a similar manner it is inadmissible on the question of the historical credibility of the gospels to conclude from historical inexactitudes concerning events which are quite at the edge of affairs that there is therefore an unreliability over central events. On this point Marxsen also argues in a manner which must be described from the point of view of the historian as inevitably leading to a false conclusion.

52 id. p. 37.   53 id. p. 39.

33

## 4. The legitimate objects of historical statements as illustrated by the Virgin Birth

The historian cannot decide by the methods used in his discipline whether the theological interpretations of the events described in the writings of the New Testament are legitimate or not. This is so even in the case of events which he accepts, after critical examination, as actually having taken place. This must be noted by way of explaining all that has previously been said. In the following chapters an attempt will be made to show by a number of examples what the historian is capable of covering, and what not.

The tidings that Jesus was born of the Virgin Mary belong to those questions about which theologians of all confessions disagree. Should this information be taken seriously in the sense of being a statement of fact, or did the Evangelist only want to stress that Jesus has a significance which extends far beyond mankind, and that Mary in a very special way 'belongs to God alone'? At first glance it would appear that the historian can say nothing about this matter. It is nevertheless worthwhile examining the texts which have been handed down from a historical point of view.

In view of the current disputes it must be stated in advance that the clarification of the literary form and tradition which has been carried out so intensely in recent times can well be extremely instructive on problems of the literary form of the text, yet have no decisive significance for the question of historical credibility, since on the one hand there are historically important pieces of information in almost all forms of literature, and on the other hand there is no literary form — not even that of pure historical narration — which guarantees that only that which is historically pertinent is reported. The same can be said of the use of certain phrases, expressions, and artifices. Evidence that Tacitus in his 'Germania' took over numerous expressions from Thucydides,

34

and that Einhart used sentences from Sveton for his biography on Karl der Große, significant as it may be for philological studies, yet it decides so very little as to whether or not anything historically significant is reported through these borrowed phrases and sentences. Willi Marxsen quite rightly stresses that 'The result of the study of historical form must not be confused with a historical judgement of the contents of the fragments handed down.'[54]

That means that conclusions on the historical credibility of the reports of His childhood cannot be drawn, either from the disputed statement that they may well be Midrashim, or from the fact that from a number of passages parallels may be drawn from the Old Testament and its associated literature.[55] On the other hand it is of greater importance that the distance in time between the actual happenings and the recording of the stories of His childhood is greater than in the reports on Jesus' public appearances and His death. There are roughly seven or eight decades between the birth of Jesus and the final written fixation of the stories of His childhood. Above all, though, we must reckon with the fact that the oral fixation began relatively late. It is unlikely that it happened before Jesus had received general recognition. That means that even the oral fixation does not lie earlier than four decades after the events. For this reason we must reckon with a relatively greater unreliability concerning the accounts of His childhood, in the sense of historical credibility. It is hard to distinguish in the childhood accounts what arises from a genuine oral tradition, and what is added later.

A comparison of the reports given by Matthew and Luke brings to light considerable variations. For the most part they do not actually have the character of incompatible contradictions. Rather, the one Evangelist reports on matters about which the other one is silent, and vice versa. Thus the scene of the proclamation by the Archangel Gabriel is only to be found in Luke, while the story of the Magi, of the star in the east, and of the murder of the firstborn by Herod only appear in Matthew. The stories of His childhood have a longer tradition behind them

54 Marxsen, Willi, Anfangsprobleme der Christologie, Gütersloh, Fourth Edition 1966, p. 11.
55 This fact as such is more or less accepted by almost all of today's exegetists in the abstract.

before they were fixed orally, and before they were noted down. It can be assumed with safety that Luke had come across the accounts as completed stories. Luke had firmly decided, 'as one who has gone over the whole course of these events in detail, I have decided to write a connected narrative for you, so as to give you authentic knowledge about the matters of which you have been informed'.[56] The question as to where these accounts originate or who gave them to the Evangelists, and by whom they were arranged and fixed in their oral form, will in all probability never be answered with absolute certainty. There is much to be said for the view that the Luke accounts go back to information supplied directly or indirectly by Mary.

As has already been mentioned, there are only a few facts which the two accounts of His childhood have in common. The most important of these are:

1. The birthplace of Jesus is Bethlehem; the later home of the family is Nazareth.
2. The mother of Jesus is Mary, the foster-father is Joseph.
3. The conception of the child does not ensue through a man, but through the Holy Ghost.

In view of these findings one could assume that one could not possibly make a sure statement from a historical point of view. Naturally one can confirm the names of Mary and Joseph, as they are named later in the Gospels. The same applies to the place of residence, Nazareth. It is more difficult with the place of birth, Bethlehem. There are theologians who take the view that the birthplace Bethlehem only appears in the accounts of His childhood because one wanted to set down the birth of Jesus as the fulfilment of old promises. Hence the statement in Matthew, 'Bethlehem in the land of Judah, you are far from least in the eyes of the rulers of Judah; for out of you shall come a leader to be the shepherd of my people Israel.'[57]

This explanation sounds plausible at first. On closer examination it is clear that the probability is not as great as many theologians assume. For anyone who explains the announcement of the birth in Bethlehem by the simple fact that Matthew wanted to emphasize the fulfilling of Old Testament sayings, misunderstands the manner in which Matthew uses Old Testament texts.

56 Luke 1, 1.    57 Matt 2, 6.

36

Willi Marxsen writes on this point, 'Now Matthew does not have a stock of Old Testament prophecies, for whose fulfilment he is searching in the events concerning Jesus. In fact he is going the other way about it. From the available passages handed down he looks out an appropriate passage in the Old Testament (a reflective quotation), which he then quotes, and thereby legitimizes the Jesus event as a fulfilment'.[58] If indeed Matthew revised this story significantly at all, it can correspondingly be assumed that he had already come across the announcement of the birth in Bethlehem and subsequently tied it up with the quotation from the Old Testament.

This opinion is supported by the fact that the accounts of Jesus' childhood also name Bethlehem as the birthplace. This assertion weighs all the heavier, as there is no dependence of the accounts given in Luke on those in Matthew. The announcement of the birth in Bethlehem must therefore have been old and generally well-known.

Finally a passage in the John Gospel can be pointed out by way of corroboration. Here it is stated, 'Others said, 'This is the Messiah.' Others again, 'Surely the Messiah is not to come from Galilee? Does not Scripture say that the Messiah is to be of the family of David, from David's village of Bethlehem? Thus he caused a split among the people.'[59] That the final compiler of the John Gospel, which has no account of Jesus' childhood, brings out the quarrel without being biassed in any way and without himself saying anything about Jesus' birthplace, also goes to show that the birthplace was firmly established in the early Christian tradition.

But that is not the question to be discussed here. Our concern is rather to see whether anything whatsoever can be said, according to the findings of these sources, about the unusual announcement, that Jesus was conceived by the Holy Ghost, and born of the Virgin Mary. At first glance it seems as if the historian must be silent and leave the field to the theologian alone.

That is a mistake, for in spite of all the difficulties, two statements can be made after a careful examination of the sources. These do not give a direct answer to the question, yet lead a step further.

Firstly the historian can state that Jesus is the son of Mary, but not the son of Joseph. This statement is already supported by the

58 Marxsen, op. cit., Introduction p. 131.    59 John 7, 41 ff.

37

fact that it occurs in two sources which are independent of each other, in Matthew and in Luke. It is confirmed by a further piece of information, namely that during the course of His public works in Nazareth, where one certainly knew roughly the family circumstances, Jesus, according to Mark's report, was called the son of Mary by his opponents. The exact words are, 'When the Sabbath came he began to teach in the synagogue; and the large congregation who heard him were amazed and said, 'Where does he get it from?', and, 'What wisdom is this that has been given him?', and, 'How does he work miracles? Is not this the carpenter, the son of Mary?'[60]

It is worthwhile examining those words, 'Is not this the carpenter, the son of Mary?' more closely. Just as with us, so among the Jews, it was generally speaking only customary at that time to name the mother of the child and not the father when the child was born out of wedlock.[61] At that time the father's, or alternatively the mother's name took the place of our family name. The question, 'Is that not the son of Mary?' means in all clarity, 'Is that not the illegitimate child of Mary?' How repugnant that precise wording was for the readers at that time is also shown by the fact that both Luke and Matthew, both of whom build up on the Mark text, have changed this passage, each in his own way, as they did not wish to impose the original text on their readers.

The above passage is of great importance in dealing with our question, since it is to be found in Mark, that is, in the oldest Gospel, and because the accounts of His childhood as given by Luke and by Matthew were not available at the time of the compilation of the Mark Gospel. It is not possible that Mark was influenced here by one of the other Evangelists.

As an argument against the virgin birth of Jesus it is occasionally pointed out that Paul, in his Letter to the Galatians,

60 Mark 6, 2. Stauffer, E. refers specifically to this passage. It is not necessary for me to offer an opinion on this debatable question, since the question is important for the problem of the semper-virginity, but not for the Virgin Birth.
61 Of course it is possible to refer to the point that the mother is every so often named even if the father has been dead for some time and is now hardly known. In the Mark text which is quoted there is, however, the expression 'Son of Mary', which is clearly used in a polemic connection, so that a so harmless interpretation is not applicable. This is confirmed not least by the modification which the text experiences in Luke and Matthew.

refers to the mother of Jesus not as a virgin, but as a woman, and that in other passages in the New Testament Joseph is 'quite impartially' referred to as the father, and more to the point, is given in the family tree at the beginning of Matthew as the 'husband of Mary'.

If one turns to the relevant passages, then the following wording is to be found in the Letter to the Galatians, 'but when the term was completed, God sent his own Son, born of a woman, born under the law . . .'.[62] If the Greek word 'Gyne', which is used here, were in fact used in every case to designate a married woman, then this passage could indeed be quoted against the virginity of Mary. That is in no way the case. The entry in Liddell+Scott's Greek-English Lexicon 62a reads: *ΓΥΝΗ, ἡ,* gen. *γυναικός,* acc. *γυναῖκα,* voc. *γύναι;* pl. *γυναῖκες, γυναικῶν,* etc., (as if from *γύναιξ*): a woman, Lat. femina, opp. to man: vocat. *γύναι,* a term of respect, mistress, lady: Homer often joins it with a second Subst., *γυνὴ ταμίη, δέσποινα,* etc. II. a wife, spouse. III. a mortal woman, opp. to a goddess. IV. the female, mate of animals.

With this knowledge in mind, if one reads the Letter to the Galatians through again, and brings in other comparable passages in Paul's Letters, then there can be no doubt that Paul, who stands fast on Jesus being the Son of God, wanted to underline the real human aspect of Jesus by this reference in the Letter to the Galatians. For he stressed that Jesus was born of an earthly woman, and was subject to Jewish law. It is thereby clear that this passage cannot be used in any critical scrutiny as an argument against the Virgin Birth.

If one then turns to the family tree in the Matthew Gospel, one can see that no argument against the Virgin Birth can be found here, but rather the contrary, that the special relationship between Joseph and Mary is confirmed. Apart from Mary there are only four women, Tamar, Rahab, Ruth, and 'the wife of Uriah' who are named in the family tree. All these cases are not concerned with normal marital relationships, but with special

---

62 Gal 4, 4.
62a In the German edition Pape's Greek-German Dictionary is quoted.
    'Gyne — (a) the womann as opposed to the man, without regard to age,
        *and irrespective of whether she is married or not;*
        (b) mortal woman as opposed to a goddess;
        (c) the married woman, the wife.'

cases. The very fact that Mary is named at all in the family tree, indicates a special relationship. In the precise wording of the family tree in Matthew, according to the contemporary view, the procreating man is given as the decisive person, and not the woman who bore the child. It begins, 'Abraham was the father of Isaac, Isaac of Jacob . . .'[63] etc. In contrast to this it is simply and solely said of Joseph, not that Jesus comes from him, but that he was the husband of Mary 'of whom Jesus was born'.[64] There is no direct connection of any sort mentioned between Joseph and Jesus.

If consideration is also given to the point that, in addition to the texts of the New Testament, there were also controversial Jewish writings before the year 70, which speak of Jesus as the 'bastard of a married woman',[65] then the historian must state that, according to the whole body of evidence from all sources, Jesus is indeed the son of Mary, but that he is not the son of Joseph. It is therefore not possible to make out of Joseph, Mary, and Jesus a kind of normal bourgeois family. All sources are agreed that there is some sort of special state of affairs in the family relationships.

The second point is that the account of the procreation by virtue of the Holy Ghost obviously did not arise through a transmission of mythical Hellenic thought, as is maintained by some theologians. The language and the whole sequence of the childhood stories speak against such an assumption. The presentation itself in the Gospels also has a different structure to that in comparable Greek and Egyptian myths. In Greek myths the god draws near to the appropriate woman in the shape of a bull, a swan, or even a golden cloud of dust, therefore in a material shape. In an Egyptian myth Ammon unites with the virgin queen in the form of the reigning king.[66] We know from several accounts even priests of the temple have occasionally assumed the role of the appropriate god in a most doubtful manner, after they had assured the woman that the god, in the form of a man, wished to unite with her. Conception takes place therefore in the Hellenic world of imagination through a material uniting of the

63 Matt 1, 2.
64 Matt 1, 16 f.
65 cf. Stauffer, E., Jesus, Dalp 332, p. 23.
66 cf. Kilian, R., Jungfrauengeburt, KBW Stuttgart 1970, especially p. 33.

god with the woman, whereby the god can assume the most varied shapes.[67]

In complete contrast it is said in Matthew, 'Mary his mother was betrothed to Joseph; before their marriage she found that she was with child by the Holy Spirit.'[68] And Luke gives the words of the angel, 'The Holy Spirit will come upon you, and the power of the Most High will overshadow you; and for that reason the holy child to be born will be called "Son of God".'[69] And he lets Mary use those well-known words, 'I am the Lord's servant; as you have spoken, so be it.'[70]

The structure of the accounts in the Gospels is therefore quite different from that of the myth. In order to make this point clear, here is the same report as it might very well have been if it were based on the myth, 'After Mary had accepted the offer of marriage, behold, the heavens opened, and the Holy Ghost came down into her lap in the form of a dove, and she conceived her son.' Yet that is not what it says at all. Instead Luke uses the expression 'by virtue of the Almighty' as a mark of the way in which God works. In his Gospel it is the 'word' of God which affects the creation by its own power and might. This is similar to the account of the creation in the Old Testament.

To sum up it can be stated that the text of the New Testament itself gives no indication of any sort that the announcement of the birth through the Virgin Mary can be taken in any other way than that reported in the childhood stories. In addition, the theme that Mary should be characterized as 'belonging to God alone', because of the word 'virgin', does not admit of confirmation from the texts of the New Testament. Just as it may be said that the whole virgin concept is used in a symbolic sense in the New

67 Lohfink, Gerhard, in his 'Katechetische Blätter' (1975 p. 312), quotes a passage from Plutarch as an argument against my opinion. An Egyptian viewpoint is referred to in which it is impossible 'that the breath of the spirit of a god draws near to a woman and causes in her the embryos of Being'. Lohfink supposes that this passage is aimed at Philon of Alexandria. In Philon we do not find, in spite of his outstanding teaching of Logos, any example which justifies such a supposition. On the other hand we know from papyrus discoveries and other information that Christianity already had followers in Egypt in the first century. According to the present state of our research it is natural to suppose that Plutarch's information (he died A.D. 123) is drawn from Christian conceptions, or at least ones already influenced by Christianity.

68 Matt 1, 18.     69 Luke 1, 35.     70 Luke 1, 38.

41

Testament, in order to signify the close connection of the church or the congregation to Christ, so is it a fact that there is not one single scrap of evidence that an actual married woman is called a virgin for the sole reason that she is inwardly a disciple of God. A person who does not accept the Virgin Birth cannot make use of the text of the New Testament as a reference, but must make other reasons hold good. These reflections lead on naturally to the next chapter.

## 5. The credibility of the miracles

The doubt concerning the reality of the Virgin Birth, which was dealt with in the previous chapter, is seldom isolated, but usually goes hand in hand with a doubt about the many miracle stories which are to be found in the New Testament, and is often coupled with a doubt about the historical reality of Jesus' resurrection too. In other words the declaration of the Archangel Gabriel, 'for with God nothing will prove impossible',[71] which occurs in the story of His childhood, meets with the scepticism of modern man, who is now living in the Age of the Second Aufklärung. It seems to me to be necessary to pass a few fundamental remarks about the credibility or the non-credibility of the miracle stories.

As a preliminary it must be said that even the concept of a miracle is used in various ways. According to the testimony of the New Testament there are not only miracles worked by the power of God, but there are also demonstrations of the power of evil and the wonders of the Antichrist, which according to the words of Jesus are so impressive that even the chosen ones are in danger of being led astray.

Hence it follows that, according to the view expressed in the New Testament, no evidence for God's existence can be deduced by reference to miracles. Karl Rahner rightly emphasizes that the miracle is not a manifestation of the power of God, 'which, independent of the readiness to believe, and of belief itself, would force itself on the empty profane empiricism of mankind, and thus drive out and make impossible decisions on faith in a true and personal sense.'[72] For that reason not even the miracles performed by Jesus Christ himself compel all men to believe. And this is according to the testimony of the New Testament. Even these miracles are interpreted differently. For some they were demonstrations of God's effective mercy, and documented the

71 Luke 1, 37.
72 Rahner, Karl, Dogmatische Bemerkungen zur Jungfrauengeburt, in: Zum Thema Jungfrauengeburt, KBW, Stuttgart, 1970 p. 131.

fulfilment of the old prophetic promises; for others they were deception and the emanation of the power of evil. According to the New Testament accounts two refutations of the messianic claim are especially put forward by the opponents of Jesus. They are:

1. In the healing of a person who is born blind they bring forth the accusation that Jesus is working with organized deceit, namely that he presents a man as healed and who has his sight, who is not identical with the blind man who was sitting by the wayside, but who merely resembles him.[73]
2. On other occasions they swear that Jesus is not accomplishing his extraordinary deeds by the power of God, but through Beelzebub, the prince of the devils.[74]

The point arises from all this, that the question of the credibility or the non-credibility of the miracle stories in fact contains two questions, which have to be kept clearly separate from each other, especially from the methodical point of view.

The first question is this, 'Are there astounding occurrences which completely gainsay our common experience, and which cannot be explained by the methods known to us, in which there are indeed forces at work which we do not know of, at least at present?'

The second question is this, 'Are there any indications in the case of certain unusual and inexplicable occurrences that they must be traced back to a special activity of God?'

In the extensive literature on the subject these questions are often fused together. Another fact adds to the confusion. The theologians and their opponents — in contrast to the New Testament — have limited the concept of the miracle to those cases in which both questions must be answered positively. Even if one agrees to accept their problematic terminology one must keep both components of the overall question apart, for methodological reasons.

(a) *Are there completely inexplicable occurrences?*

The question must be clarified as to whether there are occurrences which completely contradict our common experience, and in which powers are at work of which we at the present

73 John 9, 9.    74 Mark 3, 22.

have no knowledge. This sub-question can clearly be answered positively. There are occurrences which at least up to the present day avoid all explanation.

The enigma of unusual occurrences in many cases obviously depends on the fact that we do not know in what manner spiritual forces work. Of course it can be brought forward against this precise argument that the spirit cannot be demonstrably shown to exist, and that this wording includes a risky hypothesis. This objection is not convincing though, as it can equally well be used on closer examination against the concept of matter. Nobody is able to say what matter is. Research over the last decade especially has brought about a healthy awakening on this point. What precisely should we have in mind when Einstein teaches us that, 'What appears as matter to our senses is in reality only the conglomeration of energy in a relatively narrow space.'?[75]

The more one has penetrated into the exact nature of matter in the course of the last ten years, the less has remained of what one originally conceived to be matter. The situation can best be exemplified by what was said recently at a symposium, when a participant formulated the paradoxical sentence, 'I increasingly get the impression that in the final analysis matter is only Nothing, carefully arranged.' In fact nobody knows what matter is. What we can determine about matter with certainty, are only certain qualities and behaviour patterns, whereby these qualities and patterns of behaviour are also very different for the various forms of matter, and in addition depend on the analytical methods which we use. In spite of all this no one would dream of giving up the concept of matter. For it is especially useful for making oneself relatively well understood over a certain area of reality.

Similar observations can also be made about the concept of spirit. We are not able to define spirit, and are not able to say what spirit is. Yet the spirit makes itself known, and no one is in doubt that, for example, a human being has a spirit.

For at least as long as we have not found a better conceptual system it is at least admissable for the time being, and in certain connections absolutely necessary, to ask the question as to the way in which the spirit works, and especially the way it works on matter. In attempting to answer the question we come very

75 Einstein, Albert, Infeld, Leopold, Die Evolution der Physik, rde 12, p. 162.

45

quickly to the end of what we know. We are able to say with certainty that there are apparent influences of the spirit on matter. In this connection it is only necessary to point out that modern medicine has demonstrated that human illness must be qualitatively distinguished from animal sickness, since the course of human illness is influenced to an astounding degree by the spiritual attitude of the patient. There are, for example, cases where the curability or the incurability of an illness largely depends on whether the patient is convinced of the possibility of a cure and wishes to be cured.

The effect of medicines is also dependent on the conviction and will of the patient. That also applies to such medicines where it was first assumed that they worked purely chemically. In this connection we need only call to mind the numerous experiments with placebos, in which completely ineffective 'medicines' were handed out to the test persons, and which nevertheless, in many cases, had in fact the same effects as the appropriate genuine medicines. It cannot seriously be disputed that there are remarkable reactions of the consciousness and the will on the material condition of the body. But how they arise is unexplained. The same applies more than ever to extreme manifestations, such as healing by suggestion and autosuggestion.

It is not really necessary to turn to such scientific questions which are outside the bounds of everyday experience in order to clarify the problem which we have to consider. It is sufficient to indicate that we are not in a position to say what happens from the time of my decision to perform a specific action — such as to open or close my hand — to the first demonstrable impulse; or the way in which this decision is already coupled with material impulses. We are faced here with unsolved problems, although all this is a matter of everyday experience. It becomes even more puzzling when we think of the incontestably proven ability of certain people to move material bodies with which they have no sort of material connection, by the power of their will. In this respect all those manifestations can be called to mind, which parapsychology is engaged in investigating and in registering systematically.

It is not within the bounds of these reflections to consider whether hypotheses designed to clarify this or that manifestation will successfully be put forward, or to engage in speculations as to whether one of these days this or that manifestation will be cleared up. The establishment of this fact is sufficient, namely that there are forces and possibilities of working on matter — and on the thinking of other people in a similar manner — whose existence we can demonstrate, but over whose origin we are nevertheless in the dark. So-called extrasensory perception, and all those phenomena which make it possible to receive another signalling system, can be called to mind in this connection.

One thing can, however, be said with a fair degree of certainty, and that is that with all these phenomena we are concerned with the realization of possibilities which basically exist, and not with a breach of the laws of nature, as one was once disposed to declare in the face of inexplicable occurrences.

Nowadays we are generally agreed that there are no laws of nature in the sense used in the standard sciences, and rather that the classic laws of nature merely have a statistical character. That does not mean that one cannot depend on these laws of nature. One can rely on them in the same way that there will be cars going along the main roads tomorrow. Since there are several million cars in the Federal Republic for example, the chance that all car drivers will decide tomorrow to leave their cars in the garage is so small that for all practical purposes it does not enter into our calculation. The same applies to the laws which have been formulated in the modern sciences. These laws apply in the field of Macrophysics, that is to say in that field in which in all cases a large number of atoms and molecules are at work. Although we never know how the single atom or molecule will behave, the average behaviour of this untold number can be forecast with the same certainty with which I can say that cars will be on the road tomorrow, even though I do not know what every single car owner will be doing.

The claim that cars will be on the road tomorrow can indeed come to nothing in spite of everything as the result of a completely abnormal situation. The presupposition for this is the coordination of the behaviour of all car owners. For example, an item of news can be broadcast by the mass media which gives the impulse to all car drivers to leave their cars in the garage on the morrow, or at least to avoid certain roads. The possibility that tomorrow there will be no cars en route on the main roads is not absolutely out of the question, but merely so unlikely under normal conditions that no one needs to take it into calculation.

47

The same applies to the so-called laws of nature. They are not in the strictest sense of the word 'absolutely' valid, but they are valid with so great a probability that under normal conditions one does not need to reckon with exceptions.

Nevertheless when one asks the question about abnormal occurrences, as we are doing in these reflections, we must bring the statistical structure of the laws of nature into our thinking. By way of further clarification it must firstly be remembered that the laws of nature are only valid under so-called ideal conditions; that is to say, only then when no forces are at work which have not been taken into consideration. Thus the law of gravity strictly speaking is only valid in absolute vacuum, which cannot even be simulated in an experiment.[76] The same law is, on the contrary, of course not effective — although it basically remains 'valid' if I use a piece of paper for the experiment, and switch on a fan during the experiment. In this case the normal behaviour of matter is hindered by an exterior force.

An abnormal and unlikely behaviour of matter may not only be brought about by means of exterior forces, but can also come about if the microstructure is not left to chance, but — similar to the behaviour of the car drivers — is coordinated. Everyone knows that one can change the microstructure of a piece of iron, for example, in that one strokes along over it with the strongest possible magnet, preferably always in the same direction. Thanks to a change in its microstructure the piece of iron — without one noticing any kind of change — also gets macrostructural characteristics which it did not have previously. It now stays hanging from an iron girder in the roof, from which it would previously have always fallen. This is without the aid of a glue, and against all normal expectations and all previous experience.

On a higher plane one can characterize the special nature of plants and animals, compared with lifeless matter, not least by the fact that in their own particular way they bring about the most unlikely possibilities in matter. As modern biochemistry so impressively demonstrates, nothing happens here which is impossible chemically or physically. Yet in the field of living beings possibilities are realized by means of coordinated activity, whose realization from the standpoint of non-living matter

76 cf. Weizsäcker, Carl Friedrich von, Die Tragweite der Wissenschaft, Band 1, Stuttgart, Second Edition 1966, p. 107.

cannot be reckoned with. Fortunately no one need be afraid that a stone which is lying on the road suddenly flies upwards. In contrast, the coordinated matter which is in a frog suddenly decide to spring upwards, and the compounded matter in a bird may rise effortlessly into the air.

Since the coordinations in animals and plants have definite patterns and in this sense are stabilized — which seems unlikely in view of the nature of dead matter — the human being can nevertheless see unmistakably the whole pattern of behaviour of plants and animals, and he therefore does not generally find it surprising and astonishing.

On the contrary, the behaviour of a human being can sometimes surprise us completely, for the human being is not bound by certain patterns of action and reaction, but is characterized by his freedom. His behaviour can hardly be foreseen on occasions. The matter in our body though is only subject to our free will in a limited way. For that reason our behaviour remains in many respects calculable.

If a human being was able in spite of this to control the whole of the matter in his body freely, right deep into the microstructure, he would not have the slightest difficulty in carrying out the most astounding things. He would be able to move with great speed in every direction, simply go through walls and other obstacles, set free like lightning unimaginable forces of energy, double or even triple his size by the assumption of other matter, and many more things similar to those mentioned. None of them involve breaking the laws of nature, for basically these things lie within the framework of the possibilities available in the matter of our bodies — even if we are unable to carry out these possibilities.

As parapsychology has shown, there are people who have greater ability than most of us in this direction. Some of the occurrences which have come about can be repeated at will, and in this way can be examined experimentally. Others cannot be brought about according to plan, but occur now and then in actual situations. Even the occurrences which cannot be examined under experimental conditions are nevertheless so well testified to, that they cannot be called into question.

Such manifestations and occurrences also show empirically that there are possibilities of inducing into matter, through coordinated impulses, a completely unlikely behaviour, which contradicts all normal experience. We do not know how these possibilities are brought about in each particular case. The preliminary supposition that it could be a question of electromagnetic reactions was refuted by Russian scientists.

In view of this whole situation every critical person — that means one who weighs up all sides and is not just one-sided — must acknowledge that there are occurrences which go completely against our normal experience, and that it is not responsible scientifically to declare written or oral reports non-authentic merely because abnormal and unusual occurrences are mentioned in them. This stipulation is, basically, equally valid in the case of reports of both secular and non-secular occurrences.

As opposed to the scientist, the historian has to do with single and unrepeatable occurrences in the whole range of his discipline. Thus he does not start from the point of view that there are happenings which do not occur nowadays and so cannot have happened previously, but he tends to accept as possible that which is well attested as having happened. In other words he adjusts his concepts of the possible according to the facts, and not vice versa. Following the sense of these principles the historian prefers to take into account the fact that he has no explanation for many occurrences rather than simply denying these happenings or forcing unconfirmed interpretations into a picture which is complete in itself.

Thus Tacitus who was certainly not one who searched for miracles, reports in his Histories that Emperor Vespasian, after preliminary hesitation, healed a lame person and a blind man in Alexandria in front of numerous witnesses. He concludes the report with this sentence, 'Those who were there on that occasion still tell the story, although there is no reward for a false account.'[77] As little as the historian can explain the way in which these healings came about, so little reason has he for holding the sources to be unreliable. For this reason, for example, in Hermann Bengtson's 'Outline of Roman History' this sentence can be found by way of reference to the above literature, 'In Alexandria Vespasian healed a blind person and a lame man.'[78]

The principle, which has just been illustrated, of accepting

77 Tac. hist. IV 81.
78 Bengtson, Hermann, Grundriß der römischen Geschichte, Band 1, München, 1967, p. 316.

facts even if they do not lie within the bounds of normal experience, does not exclude the point that the historian is always sceptical when the sources which report on unusual events are themselves unreliable. Philostratus for example, reports in this doubtful fashion towards the end of the third century. In a fiction-like presentation he records numerous miracles which the neopythagorian philosopher, Apollonius of Tyana in Capadocia, who was living about the time of Jesus, is supposed to have brought about. The historian displays a similar sceptiscism towards the descriptions of numerous lives of Saints, in which there are accounts of astounding miracles. Yet the historian always asks after the credibility of the sources as a whole, both in the case of the description given by Philostratus, as well as that of the legends of the Saints. Since these sources as a whole are not credible, he is also sceptical about all the miracles contained therein. He does not maintain though from the very first that certain things just could not have happened, and that every source which reports this kind of thing is therefore bad.

If one now turns, after these preliminary reflections, to the accounts of the miracles as given in the New Testament, and if one then asks after the credibility of the unusual events which are reported there, then one must at once accept certain pieces of evidence which arise from our experience of secular history. As we have previously mentioned, it does happen that someone attributes further unusual deeds to a person who has already done or performed something out of the ordinary, and it especially happens that a person varies an account or tells it with variations when dealing with things which he himself has performed, so that in the end several quite separate accounts of events arise from this. Similar ornamentations, additions, repetitions, and transfers must obviously be reckoned with in the miracle stories of the evangelists.

The origin of unhistorical additions can be accurately followed and demonstrated at several points in the Gospels. Here is one remarkable example. In the relatively oldest report of the blind man of Jericho — in the report given in the Mark Gospel — there is talk of a blind beggar who is also introduced by name as Bartimaeus, son of Timaeus.[79] In the account by Luke the matter concerns a blind man, without a name being mentioned.[80] And in

79 Mark 10, 46–52.    80 Luke 18, 35–43.

Matthew the story reads, 'At the roadside sat "two" blind men.'[81] From the context it appears that all three reports are concerned with the same happening. One can see with all clarity that a duplication of the healed person has occurred. At the same time the reports of Luke and of Matthew lose a little of their historical essence by the fact that the name is no longer reported.

If one turns to the whole problem of the miracle stories after considering this single example, then one can determine from the point of view of the historian that it is impossible in most of the accounts to decide with historical certainty whether events came to pass just as they were reported. One thing however one has to state, albeit with considerable circumspection, namely that it is not credible, and from a historical point of view impossible, that these miracle stories as a whole are the result of a free-roaming imagination. One must continuously call to mind that the oral fixation of the reports already began shortly after the actual happenings and that the final written fixation of the first Gospels was brought to a conclusion at a time when the greater part of the eyewitnesses were still living. The distance in time between the actual happenings and their final fixation in writing in the Mark Gospel is probably about the same as our distance from the Adenauer Era or from Suez, and certainly not greater than our distance in time from the Third Reich.

Completely unusual things must indeed have come to pass. Otherwise these reports would never have arisen, and above all they would otherwise have had no chance of being believed. Finally there is the additional confirmatory point that the Jewish opponents of Jesus never called into question the fact that Jesus performed extraordinary things. They merely give a completely different interpretation to them.

## (b) *Does God intervene in the working of things?*

At this point I return to the second of the questions posed. Even if one decides after a critical examination of the sources that Jesus did in fact bring about such unusual things as are reported in the Gospels, it is still not settled whether these extraordinary deeds must be referred to as miracles, worked by the power of God as the evangelists say. This second question, in contrast to the

81 Matt 20, 29–34.

52

first, cannot be approached by the methods of historical scholarship, but only by means of general scientific and theoretical considerations.

As has already been mentioned, the contemporaries disputed this point. Even modern interpreters of the Gospel have declared that Jesus performed his cures not by the power of God, but through a combination of suggestion and autosuggestion. Jesus could well have been successful in the same way as 'miracle doctors' whom the popular press report on from time to time.

Let us begin by asking a general question. Are there any indications in the course of certain unusual happenings that they can be traced back to an unusual activity on the part of God?

It must be stated beforehand that for atheists this is a non-question, for if there is no God then he cannot cause anything. As I have dealt with the question of God's existence in another book,[82] I do not wish to consider the atheist's position in connection with the present enquiry, especially as the point of view of the atheist is only represented by very few biblical scholars.

As long as one does not deny the existence of God, one has to accept the point that God has possibilities of working on material procedures which surpass in quality even that which is possible in extreme cases for the human being. Indeed one must recognize that there are fundamentally no limits of any sort to the possibilities of God's intervention. If the word 'almighty' has any meaning at all, and is not merely used as flowery language, then the possibility of influencing matter and its behaviour is also affirmed in the assertion that God is almighty. It is a remarkable fact that all that which has just been said is accepted by most theologians. Yet many theologians claim that God is basically able to work miracles, but that he does not actually do so.[83] Of course I ask myself how the theologians concerned know that. I grant that theologians, by the nature of their scholarship are nearer to God

82 Staudinger, Hugo, Gott — Fehlanzeige? op. cit.
83 According to my own observations, deistical ideas of God and the world are at work with many theologians when they seek to answer the question of the miracles. Remarks, for example, such as the one that God does not suspend laws which He himself has given, and similar ideas, belong to this category. The methical and theoretical preliminaries can be read in Staudinger/Behler, Chance und Risiko der Gegenwart, eine kritische Analyse der wissenschaftlich-technischen Welt, Paderborn 1976.

than the historian. But I am not aware that they have information which is only available to them and which allows them to state what God does do and what not.

Now that means that it cannot be excluded from the very start that unusual and to us inexplicable occurrences take place through a special intervention of God. Especially if one grants this point, one should indeed avoid attributing too hastily to God all that which cannot be explained at the moment. If many people nowadays dispute every unusual intervention of God in the things of this world, then that is not least a result of the fact that God has sometimes all too readily been inserted as a gap-filler in all those places where one did not know of any other answer.

On the other hand we must draw emphatic attention to the point that we know many things today which could not be explained even a few decades ago, and that we very probably shall be able to know many things tomorrow which we cannot explain today. In addition we have to recognize that there are inexplicable occurrences, with surrounding circumstances, where a direct tracing back to God can be almost excluded. One need only think of the greater part of parapsychic phenomena. It is as well to remember in this respect that Jesus also speaks of miracles which are not brought about by God.

Even in the case of inexplicable and remarkable occurrences which are found in the Christian connection, a critical examination is appropriate in every single case. There are two reasons for this.

1. During the Middle Ages in various places 'Holy Bread stained with blood' was worshipped. Today there are good grounds for the view that the red colouring of the Holy Bread (the Host) was due in a series of cases to the effect of a certain fungus. This red colouring was referred to by earlier people all too hastily as a miraculous manifestation, since they had no other explanation for it, and because this interpretation lay within the bounds of their own pious expectations.

2. One of the decisive battles between Islam and Christianity was as we know the sea battle of Lepanto, by means of which the Turkish Fleet lost the aura of invincibility. On the 7th October 1571 the Christian fleet, under the command of Don John of Austria, and equipped by Spain, the Republic of Venice, and Pope Pius V, gained a splendid victory in Greek waters against the

numerically superior Turks. On the very same day Pope Pius V held a conference in Rome with a number of church dignitaries. He suddenly got up during the conference, opened the window, turned round after a short while, and announced a Service of Thanksgiving for the victory. This event is so well witnessed that the historical fact is not in doubt. Yet who will decide in this case, and with absolute certainty, whether this is a case of inspiration by God, or whether we shall be able to explain this happening scientifically one of these days with the help of parapsychology, such as by a signal system which has not yet been the subject of research? For this reason I am of the opinion that a certain reticence is called for in the interpretation of this and similar occurrences.

After these warnings against a too hasty belief in miracles comes a warning with the same degree of emphasis against a short-circuiting scepticism about miracles. The following conclusions are important for our theme in this connection:

If God did reveal himself to mankind, and especially if he became true Man in Jesus Christ, then it must be accepted that those extraordinary happenings which are directly connected with the Revelation and the Incarnation, and which are historically well attested, are concerned with a special act of God. The same surely applies to Jesus' miracles, in which he shows not only human but also godly compassion towards the people who believe in him.

Quite contrary to the expectations of many of his contemporaries and even of people today the miracles which were performed by Jesus, or those which are connected with his appearance, have two specific characteristics in common: they are neither demonstrations nor sensations.

It must be pointed out in this connection that the sentence, 'for with God nothing will prove impossible' can very easily be misunderstood, and that this misunderstanding is based on the fact that we are faced with an inadequate, not to say false translation of the text. When we hear that nothing is impossible for God, then we are stimulated by this wording to put the sort of questions which are usually put by children at a certain age, 'Can God also make our car run on water?', 'Can God also make sure that I do well in my test tomorrow, even if I don't do a single thing today?', 'Can God build an escalator to the moon?', and so on.

Although it may be right for the time being to answer children of that age with a 'Yes, if he wants to', in order not to cast doubt on the Almighty Power of God, yet it would be wrong to leave the matter with this 'yes'. It would be especially wrong as an adult even to pose questions of this kind, which are inappropriate, and in this respect false ones. God is not a super-conjurer, who has to prove himself by tricks which we think out, but His Almighty Power is shown in the fact that His promises are and will be fulfilled.

I now come to the answer given by the angel to Mary, which is given in Luke. The Greek, text reads, 'οὐκ ἀδυνατήσει παρὰ τοῦ Θεοῦ πᾶν ῥῆμα'. There is no mention in this text of a 'thing', but of the 'word'.[84] This is the same Greek word which comes up again in Mary's reply, 'γένοιτό μοι κατὰ τὸ ῥῆμά σου'. (As you have spoken, so be it.) Even the statement which the angel makes using this word is not sufficiently brought out in the German — and also in the English — translation 'not impossible', for in the Greek this is a verb. The main component is the word δύναμις — might, power — that word to which our words 'dynamic' and 'dynamite' can be traced back. As the double negative of the Greek sentence translates badly into German and English, it can probably be best expressed by the sentence, 'Every word of His will be vigorously carried out by God.' It is therefore not every chance thing — thought out by us to test God — which will be fulfilled, but He will take care that His word does not remain powerless, but becomes reality.

All the Gospels with one accord report that Jesus always refuses to perform miracles if people expect a sensation or demand a demonstration. He does not cause a sign to come from Heaven, as the scribes and the pharisees demand. He does not come down from the cross, although his enemies assure Him that they would then believe Him. He does not perform a miracle in front of Herod, who would certainly have been very pleased. On the contrary Jesus shows mercy through miracles to all them who come with faith and trust to Him, and shows in the boundless compassion of God the fulfilment of the scriptures.

Jesus does not perform miracles to make life easier or to ensure well-being. When he sends his disciples out he gives them instructions to eat what is put in front of them, and he says with

84  The word is also 'Verbum' in the Vulgate version.

emphasis that the labourer is worthy of his hire. He also calls upon them to shake the dust off their feet where they are not wanted. Yet he does not give each of them a vade-mecum[84a], so as to guarantee their livelihood, and to make clear to reluctant people on the spot what they have deserved.

In Canaan he does turn water into wine for those who have no more, but so that they can continue to be joyful, and he gives enough bread to eat to all those who follow Him and hear His word. But nevertheless when they want to make Him king in order to safeguard their own livelihood on a long-term basis he flees and hides himself.

Even the Coming of Jesus to Paul who persecuted him is, in my opinion, misunderstood, that is, if it is called a demonstration of might towards a man who will not acknowledge this same might. Paul believes in God, and Paul is convinced that he is doing a service to God by persecuting Christians. Even before his conversion Paul wants to carry out the will of God in all things. That is why he asks for the full power of authority from the high priests, and why he goes to Damascus. When Jesus appears to this man, then he is only helping him towards that which he was wanting to do all the time; namely to serve God and His will.

If all these facts are kept in mind then it seems likely that a part of the present-day scepticism is quite rightly turned against the representation of God as a super-conjurer whom we can call upon at any time to perform this or that trick, and indeed who owes it to us to prove His reality in this way if we feel inclined, for any old reason, to call His reality into question.

The rejection of all unseemly conceptions of the effectiveness of Almighty God should certainly not be transformed into a factual denial of this allpowerfulness. In so far as the individual believes in God at all, he should nowadays recognize that God embodies His will at times in a sovereignty which surpasses our imagination. He can above all refer on this matter to the point that God, even in our own days, as authentic documents show, is still working in sovereign freedom when and where He will. On

84a  The German words at this point refer to folk-lore tales which suggest helpful self-sufficiency. There is a table which replenishes itself, a donkey which ejects golden coins, and a stick which comes out of a sack at a given command and beats its owner across the back if he shows signs of flagging.

this point reference need only be made to Wilhelm Schamoni's book 'Miracles are Facts',[85] which documents the miracles in Lourdes and in other places.

## (c) Bultmann's Interpretations of the Miracles. An Excursus

The credibility of the gospel miracle stories is confirmed not least by the very manner of arguing, the argumentation with which Bultmann seeks to shake them. His argumentation is not acceptable from the point of view of scholarship. The story of the healing of the blind man in Jericho, which has already been mentioned, is just one example. Rudolf Bultmann's account reads, 'The blind Bartimeus. The story is thereby revealed as of secondary importance in that the blind man is given a name (see below); it is the sole name in a synoptic miracle story apart from Mark 5, 22 (see below). Nevertheless it is possible that the name, which is missing in Matthew and Luke, was inserted later in Mark.'[86]

In the later passage, to which Bultmann refers, he writes, 'On some occasion in the course of time an anecdotal interest was awakened concerning the persons involved in miracle stories. The Haimorrhoissa (the woman with the haemorrhage) for example, received the name Veronica (e.g.: Evg. Nicodemus 7) and became an Edessian princess in Macarius Magn. 16. The woman of Phoenicia and her daughter are called Justa and Berenice according to Clement (Hom II, 19; III, 73). We also remember how the man who was awakened from the dead in the Lazarus story (John 11), and his sisters, all bear names, whilst the 'young man from Nain' and his mother are unnamed in Luke. This anecdotal tendency can already be observed in the synoptic gospels. The president of the synagogue (Luke 8, 41) is given the name Jairus, which has also forced its way into most of the Mark 5, 22 manuscripts (see above p. 230). With such a state of affairs one is sceptical about the name Bartimeus in Mark 10, 46.'[87]

Regarding this sort of argumentation, the following needs

---

85 Schamoni, W., Wunder sind Tatsachen, eine Dokumentation aus Heiligsprechungsakten, Naumann Verlag Würzburg, 1976.
86 Bultmann, Synoptische Tradition, op. cit. p. 228.
87 id. p. 256.

first of all to be stated: Bultmann is right in that in narrative stories names are occasionally added out of anecdotal interest. There is also the opposite process though which we all know from our everyday experience, namely that the names of persons who only appear briefly are quickly forgotten. This is also our experience when we recall only too well certain happenings which are connected with those persons. We all tell stories, of encounters and events on our holiday travels, in hospital, at meetings or on other occasions, by first mentioning the one name or the other. After a short time these names are left out. The events are from now on reported without the names, which are indeed, as we say, 'beside the point'. Bultmann does not mention this process which occurs so frequently, but gives the impression either consciously or unconsciously that the naming of a name arises in every case from an anecdotal interest and is thus in every case a sign of relatively later items of tradition.

He begins the presentation of evidence with reference to the woman who is healed of the flow of blood and who receives the name Veronica in the later tradition, and the fact that the later tradition calls the woman from Phoenicia and her daughter by the names of Justa and Berenice. These examples can quite rightly be quoted by Bultmann in support of his theory that there is, very early within the Christian tradition, 'an anecdotal interest in the persons involved in the miracle stories' which leads to a subsequent addition of names. In the case of both of these examples it is not a matter, though, of the addition of names in the gospel texts themselves. The following examples do indeed concern such an addition.

Bultmann writes, 'We also recall how the man who was awakened from the dead in the Lazarus story (John 11), and his sisters, all bear names, whilst the 'young man from Nain' and his mother are unnamed in Luke.' Bultmann overlooks the point that we are concerned here with occurrences which are hardly comparable, apart from both being raisings from the dead. According to the Luke account Jesus meets the widow of Nain and her son on one single occasion — we might almost say by chance — without ever having met them before.

On the other hand, in the case of Lazarus and his sisters we are concerned, according to the account in John, with a family with whom Jesus was 'friendly'. In view of the differences in the degree of acquaintanceship the mention of the names in the Lazarus story yields nothing really in the sense of scholarly reasoning about the question under discussion.

What about the next name on Bultmann's list, namely Jairus? Bultmann writes, 'This anecdotal tendency can already be observed in the synoptic gospels. The president of the synagogue (Luke 8, 41) is given the name Jairus, which has also forced its way into most of the Mark 5, 22 manuscripts.' Not much can be done with the theory that the name of Jairus, taken from Luke, has 'forced its way' into most of the Mark manuscripts, if it is not possible to find out the degree of probability in Bultmann's supposition. There is a definite scholarly method for that, which certainly was not used by Bultmann. We seek to find out whether the source findings can also be explained by other theories which are just as plausible or even more so.

If we apply this method to the question of the name of Jairus, then the opposite theory follows, that the name of Jairus was to be found from the very beginning in Mark, but subsequently it was not written down by one or other copyist, whether through oversight, or because the man seemed to have been identified enough by his title of president of the synagogue. Since Luke, as opposed to Matthew, used one of the unchanged manuscripts as the model for his work, he of course took over the name Jairus into his own gospel.

We would all agree that this assumption is more obvious as it does not provoke the question, as Bultmann's theory does, as to why the name of Jairus has not 'forced its way' into the manuscripts of the Matthew gospel. The theory that the name of Jairus was originally not to be found in the Mark text cannot be substantiated by scholarship. It is even highly improbable. The case of Jairus cannot therefore support Bultmann's whole theory.

We now come to the last link in Bultmann's chain of evidence. He writes, 'Under these circumstances we become sceptical about the name Bartimaeus (Mark 10, 46) . . .' 'The story (of the blind man in Jericho) is thus revealed as of secondary importance, since the blind man is named by name . . . It is the only name in a miracle story apart from Mark 5, 22 . . . It is hardly possible to recognize an original miracle story, told in the same style, as the basis.' The admission of this example already shows a certain capriciousness in Bultmann's chain of argumentation, for the name is found in Mark, that is in the oldest gospel, whilst it is missing in Luke and Matthew.

By way of clarification it is worthwhile making a counter-check and to search for a better explanation of the text finding than the one given by Bultmann. It could go like this, 'The Mark account of the blind Bartimaeus, son of Timeus, can be seen to be old and reliable by the fact that here, as opposed to the great majority of the miracle stories in the synoptic gospels, the name of the blind beggar is also given, a name which is not important for the purposes of the story, whereas later Luke and Matthew do without the name, which is 'beside the point'. The fact that the report is not approximated to other miracle stories in the manner of telling speaks for the genuineness and the originality of the story.'

In fact this explanation is more plausible than the tortuous theories of Bultmann, especially if we call to mind how early the Mark Gospel took on a firm shape, and how little the anecdotal interest is otherwise traceable in it. The postscript, which is conceived of by Bultmann as being his utmost concession, 'Nevertheless it is possible that the name, which is missing in Matthew and Luke, was inserted later in Mark' can only be described as the result of an uncritical phantasy. Does Bultmann in all seriousness want to make the point ring true that later copyists, just out of 'anecdotal interest', inserted the name Bartimaeus, son of Timeus, in all the Mark texts which were then available, whilst they also scrupulously avoided undertaking the same insertion in the Luke text and Matthew text? Even if we accept that imaginative speculation has its legitimate place in scholarship, and that it has often been the pointer to learned knowledge, we cannot get round the point that in this particular instance Bultmann has gone considerably beyond the bounds which are acceptable in a learned discussion.

Reference should also be made to the point that, according to Bultmann's theory, it must be expected that more names are to be found in the gospels which were drawn up later than in the earlier ones. In fact the very opposite is the case. The John Gospel, which was finally fixed latest, includes the least names, both in actual numbers and also in the percentage of its length. On the other hand the short Mark Gospel — also the oldest gospel — taken in absolute figures, contains just as many names as the Matthew

Gospel which is 70% longer. The number of names is only exceeded by the number in the longest gospel, which is in my opinion the relatively early Luke Gospel. This point does not mean anything conclusive since the amount of narrative material and speeches in the gospels is variably distributed. Nevertheless this rough statistical estimate tells right from the start against the views put forward by Bultmann.

From this detailed treatment of a single example the following general indications of the manner in which Bultmann puts forward his arguments may be stated.

1. Bultmann collects an abundance of material together in the discussion of Jesus' miracles, as well as on other occasions. He neglects however to check his material critically and to process it. The following is an example, 'The procedure whereby miracle stories which are already existent and other anecdotes are applied to a hero, a saviour, or a god, can often be observed in the history of a literature or of a religion. I quote Ovid Metamorphoses VI, 313 *et seq.* as an example, where the theme of the farmers being turned into frogs is transfered to Latona; it was originally a popular story which was told by an old witch, as it is told in Apuleius, Metamorphosis XII. In 'The Thousand-and-One Nights' Harun al Raschid became a hero or a player of parts in numerous fairy stories . . .'[88]

The introductory statement of this Bultmann quotation is certainly correct, but even the first example is absolutely inapplicable as an argument; it is absolutely unsuitable if we bear in mind that the example is not concerned with historical persons, so that it misses the point entirely as a comparison to Jesus. The second example is relevant in so far as Harun al Raschid is a historical personality. Yet this example also leads to false conclusions. For Bultmann does not call attention to the fact that Harun al Raschid died shortly after 800 and that the tales from 'Thousand-and-One Nights' were first recorded in their present form in the fifteenth century. As soon as this additional point is made, it becomes clear that even this example says nothing at all about the early Jesus tradition.

2. Bultmann tends to generalize special cases. Here is a specific example, 'The miracles are as it were something detached from His individual willing, something functioning automatic-

88 id. p. 244.

ally. This is especially clear in the story of the Haimorhoissa. Jesus feels, after the woman touched Him, that a δύναμις went out of Him.'[89]

The story of the woman with the flow of blood is almost unique though.[90] With most of the miracles we are concerned with almost everything else except things which function automatically. In addition the story of the Haimorhoissa itself need not be interpreted at all in the way in which Bultmann proposes. In my opinion the following interpretation is just as applicable:

In view of the great crowd the woman with the flow of blood is too shy to turn beseechingly to Jesus with her special illness. Besides, this woman — I agree with Bultmann on this point — has a magical notion of the wonderful healing power of Jesus. She therefore touches His clothes in the expectation of being automatically healed without attracting attention. The required healing does in fact come about. In that Jesus turns round and speaks to her, He at the same time enlightens her that His healings do not take place in the sense of magical automatic reactions, but that He is rather the knowing master of the powers which go out from Him.

3. Bultmann tends to formulate risky speculations as incontestable statements. As an example, attention need only be called to two statements which are to be found, together with a number of further statements, on one single page:

(a) Bultmann writes, 'Mark 3, 1–5, Luke 13, 10–17, and 14, 1–6 are thus only variations of the theme of Sabbath healing.'[91] Anyone who takes the trouble to turn up the texts must reach the conclusion that the parallel to Mark 3, 1–5 is found in Luke 6, 6–11, and that the stories of the healing on the other hand in Luke 13, 10–17 and Luke 14, 1–6 do not create the impression of being 'only variations of the theme of Sabbath healings'. If one were to work so rashly with a variation theory in secular history, one would reach completely nonsensical conclusions.

We can observe that historical disputes often concern certain key questions which occur again and again. This is the case — to

89 id. p. 234.
90 Mark 6, 56 is comparable. Even in this passage there are magical thoughts, yet the general formulation of the ideas gives no clear answer to the question whether this magical way of thinking by Jesus is to some extent accepted.
91 Bultmann, Synoptische Tradition, op. cit., p. 242.

name one example taken from secular history — with the various disputes between Emperor Friedrich Barbarossa and the Italian cities about fundamental questions concerning an agreed limitation of rights and duties. What a gross distortion would one achieve in history if one considered the reports of these abundant and repeated disputes as only variations of the one and the same historical event? We can say in any case that within historical happenings certain fundamental problems crop up with ever-fresh variations. That means to say that it is not the recorders who subsequently vary a single happening again and again, but that the historical events are themselves variations of certain fundamental themes. This very structure is obviously the subject of the varying reports about the disputes between Jesus and the Pharisees with whom the question of healing on the sabbath was in question.

(b) The following apodictic wording is just as incongruous. 'The miracle of the healing of the ten lepers Luke 17, 7–19 is an increasing variation of Mark 1, 40–45, as the command Luke 17, 14 especially demonstrates, ἐπιδείξατε ἑαυτοὺς τοῖς ἱερεῦσιν (Go and show yourself to the priests).'[92] It must firstly be pointed out, in order to judge the whole finding, that Luke (5, 12–16) takes over the story of the healing of the lepers from Mark, and that Luke himself certainly did not make up this 'increasing variation'. Otherwise the report on the ten lepers would have to turn up in the passage in the account of the one leper, in the same way as the healing of the two blind men of Jericho occurs in Matthew, instead of the story about the healing of the one blind man.

In addition, the sentence, 'Go and show yourself to the priests' which does not take into account the situation of the Samaritans, does not prove that here there is a variation of the whole tale, which differs considerably from the story of the healing of the single leper. A comparison soon shows this. Since it was a definite and general instruction in the Old Testament that persons healed of leprosy had to present themselves to the priests, these sayings can come into the story in a purely formal manner; or perhaps, under the circumstances, have been included by assimilation with Luke 5, 14. This can, indeed, no more be proved than the hypothesis of Bultmann.

4. Bultmann is of the erroneous opinion that historical

92 id. p. 242.

developments take a straightforward course, and happen according to rule. He writes, 'The greater part of the history of the Tradition lies in the dark; a small part can be observed by means of sources, namely the modification which the Mark material experienced in the processing by Matthew and Luke. With all due consideration for the question of the Original-Mark, which plays a role at this point, and of the problems of textual criticism, which do not permit a sure judgement in every case, a certain regularity can nevertheless be observed in the handling of Mark by Matthew and Luke. We are dependent on Matthew and Luke for the reconstruction of Q; but also here, by a comparison of Q with Matthew and Luke, it can be recognized to what rules the continuity of material from Q to Matthew and Luke was subjected. If such a conformity can really be determined, then one may assume that it was already effective on the Tradition material before its fixation in Mark and Q, and so one can reason *a posteriori* back to an earlier stage of the Tradition than that which is fixed in our sources . . .'[93]

In the above passage Bultmann sets himself two tasks:

(a) to determine the inherent evolution with which the history of the Tradition was accomplished in the period between the fixing of the Mark Gospel and the fixing of the Matthew or Luke Gospel, and

(b) from thence to draw inferences about the history of the Tradition before the written fixation in Mark and in Source Q.

The first of these two tasks is already more difficult than it would seem from Bultmann's exposition. For it can only be said with certainty in a few passages that Luke or Matthew undertook changes from the Mark text for the further development of their own material. In most cases the possibility cannot be excluded that they undertook the changes under the influence of variations which are no longer extant and whose tradition and age we simply do not know.

As I have already remarked, there were probably more texts available to the compilers of the main gospels than most theologians assume. By means of a systematic examination of all parallel and double speeches, as well as changes in the text order, this theme could in all probability be shown to be the correct one.

93 id. p. 7.

In that case very special attention would have to be paid to those passages in which the Luke text or the Matthew text is apparently, or even possibly, nearer the events than the Mark text. It is a significant thing that Bultmann always comes across passages in which he considers the Luke or the Matthew text more original than the Mark text which, seen as a whole, is essentially the older one. A certain degree of caution is advisable when we begin to formulate the inherent evolutions of the Tradition history. The Mark text need not be the more original in every case.

The attempt by Bultmann to draw the conclusion about an even 'earlier stage of the Tradition' by comparisons between texts which are in part available to us and in part hypothetical, is especially problematic. It is indeed more than dubious according to the criteria used in historical studies. For the assumptions of Bultmann that the same inherent evolution which characterizes a later stage of the history of the Tradition also applies to the earlier stages is demonstrably false.

By way of clarification let us once again recall the story of the healing of the blind man of Jericho. Bultmann allowed himself to be led into making a false judgement in that he projected the anecdotal tendency, which in fact comes at a later stage of development according to the wording of the gospels, and which can be demonstrated by a whole row of examples, into the period of the composition of the gospels. We need only refer to that which has already been said on this subject.

The history of the Tradition, as in those miracle stories which he deals with in connection with the sayings of Jesus, is similarly inappropriately drawn to pattern. Two conceptions play a role in this; the conception of the Apophthegma, the apophthegms, which Bultmann describes as stories, 'whose point lies in a narrow word-picture of Jesus, which is presented in a short scene;'[94] there is also the conception of the ideal scene, which is characterized by the fact that it demonstrates a truth which goes beyond the concrete connection.

It is characteristic of Bultmann's conceptual structures that he also constructs alternatives which are far from reality. He writes:

(a) 'a biographical apophthegma is by its very nature just not a

94 id. p. 8.

historical report, neither for Jesus nor for any other personality in history.'[95]

(b) 'An ideal scene is one which can be described as having its origin, not in an historical event, but one which has an idea which is to be illustrated in the form of a picture.'[96]

Both statements are however narrowed down by Bultmann in different ways in view of the impossibility of actually sustaining them. Thus he concedes, for example, that, 'Naturally an historical recollection can be included in such stories.'[97] He declares further concerning the one or the other tale that it is 'probably (concerned with) an historical event'.[98]

Unfortunately it is not possible in these short reflections to express an opinion on the numerous detailed interpretations by Bultmann. Fundamentally though, I would like to note the following points concerning Bultmann's key expressions, namely Apophthegma and the Ideal Scene. Obviously an apophthegm does not of necessity have to reproduce an historical saying, but can be thought up out of real literary pleasure in expressing the pregnant form. The same applies to the ideal scene, whereby there is a flowing transition between the apophthegm and the ideal scene. But the statement which is so played up by Bultmann, namely that we are not dealing thereby with historical reports, is only a half-truth.

In history there have always been personalities who gave striking and pregnant answers on the appropriate occasion, and so became key figures in ideal scenes. By the manner of their behaviour and by their answers they turned real scenes into ideal ones. In this respect we only need to recall famous sayings of Caesar such as 'The dice has fallen', You are riding Caesar and his luck', or 'Rather be the first here than the second in Rome'. The many sayings of Tallyrand, together with the appropriate scene, could just as well be quoted. A word from Freiherr vom Stein on that point, 'In the very moment of a general misfortune it would be very immoral to bring one's own personality into the reckoning.'

These and many other scenes are — in that I agree with Bultmann — scenes which are on the one hand complete in themselves and assertive; on the other hand though — and this

95 id. p. 60.     96 id. p. 48 note 3.     97 id. p. 60.     98 id. p. 59.

Bultmann overlooks — they are at the same time scenes which belong in a historical context. The connection is demonstrable in most scenes; in others it is the subject of dispute; and in yet others it can be shown that they were only subsequently included in the framework which we now have.

As a rule, in the first stage of the Tradition the scene is reported in its correct historical context. In the second stage impressive scenes or sayings are handed on in isolation. In the third stage a part of these scenes is finally included in a new — but unhistorical — framework. New scenes, moreover, are made up and added on occasions. Agreed, not all parts of the Tradition pass through all three stages. Not only that, but the tempo of the development is variable.

In the gospels it must be correspondingly reckoned with that there are scenes which have been handed down in their historically original connection, as well as others which have subsequently been inserted into context. Unhistorical additions must moreover be reckoned with, in which case it must be taken into account that the oral and written fixation happened at an early date, so that in cases of doubt the probability speaks for the earlier stage of development.

Bultmann does not do the stratification of this historical development justice, but presses everything into one pattern. This learned *tour de force* then looks something like this:

(a) At the end of the story which tells how Jesus came into conflict with the Pharisees over the plucking of the ears of corn on the Sabbath, Mark says, 'On another occasion when he went to the synagogue, there was a man in the congregation who had a withered arm; and they were watching to see whether Jesus would cure him on the Sabbath, so that they could bring a charge against him. He said to the man with the withered arm, 'Come and stand out here.' Then he turned to them: 'Is it permitted to do good or to do evil on the Sabbath, to save life or to kill?' They had nothing to say; and, looking round at them with anger and sorrow at their stupidity, he said to the man, 'Stretch out your arm.' He stretched it out and his arm was restored. But the Pharisees, on leaving the synagogue, began plotting against him with the partisans of Herod to see how they could make away with him.'[99]

99 Mark 3, 1 ff.

Bultmann has this to say, 'The buildup is compact. The redaction has not provided a special introduction ... The last verse however ... is a redactional addition, for it betrays the biographical interest which is otherwise foreign to the disputes and learned discussions, and does not meet the point of the story, namely the question of principle in the healing on the Sabbath.'[100]

At this point it becomes abundantly clear that Bultmann in the course of his deliberations only has the later stages of development of the Tradition in mind. He considers the reports always as mere originally isolated stories, and overlooks that they are set in a concrete situation in the first stage of development.

Of course it is not possible to provide a positive scholarly proof that in the case in question the final verse formed part of the story from the very beginning. Yet it is just as inadmissable to consider it as pure editorial work simply because it mentions a larger context in which the account of the healing occurs. Such a finding can equally well indicate that this part of the Tradition has been simply handed down in the first stage of development. Such an assumption is justified in all cases where important reasons do not demand the opposite. For the overall interest of the compilers of the New Testament writings — and this already applies to the compilers of the oral tradition — is not devoted to the Apophthegma or the ideal scene for their own sakes, but applies to the unique person Jesus who stands at the centre of their whole thought. For the man or woman who is interested in the person Jesus the final verse is in that case of special significance.

(b) Mark reports, 'Jesus was walking by the shore of the Sea of Galilee when he saw Simon and his brother Andrew on the lake at work with a casting-net; for they were fishermen. Jesus said to them, 'Come with me, and I will make you fishers of men.' And at once they left their nets and followed him. When he had gone a little further he saw James son of Zebedee and his brother John, who were in the boat overhauling their nets. He called them; and, leaving their father Zebedee in the boat with the hired men, they went off to follow him.'[101]

Bultmann writes about this passage thus, 'Both sections vary the same theme ... The theme is the sudden calling forth to be a 'successor' ... No word of explanation is necessary to show that this is not a historical report, but a matter of an ideal scene.'[102] The

100 Bultmann, p. 9.     101 Mark 1, 16 ff.     102 Bultmann, p. 27.

69

short-circuitry of the Bultmann argumentation is hereby shown. That which is an ideal scene cannot be, in his opinion, at the same time a real scene. Of course we must accept that even in this particular case the one or the other scene can be unhistorical. But that must then be made credible in detail. The apodictic assurance of Bultmann, 'No word of explanation is necessary to show that this is not a historical report, but a matter of an ideal scene' is thus in any case untenable.

5. Without demonstrating precisely, even by a single example, that a certain miracle has come into the gospels through the takeover from another tradition, Bultmann offers an over-rich abundance of traditions outside the Bible in which there could well have been a taking over. In many places he creates the impression that such a takeover is hardly in doubt. A few examples of Bultmann's procedure can be quoted here:

(a) Bultmann writes, 'There were also stories of wonderful feedings in the Hellenic world. Thus Celsus (orig. c. C. I. 68) reports that heathen workers of miracles also brought about miraculous feedings.'[103] Bultmann himself should know how questionable such a reference is. For Celsus is for his part polemically dependent on the gospels, and not vice versa! It is well-known that Celsus composed his disputation against the Christians in the year 179 after Christ, that is to say roughly a hundred years after the written fixation of the gospels.

(b) Bultmann writes, 'At least one further example can be given of the way in which Hellenistic miracle stories forced their way into the Christian tradition at a later date, namely the miracle of the wine at the wedding in Cana (John 2, 1–12) which demonstrates the transfer of the epiphany feast of Dionysos to

103 Bultmann, Synoptische Tradition, p. 251. It is worth noting, by the way, that Celsus is also 'inserted' in a rather curious way by other exegetists. Lohfink, on p. 125 f. of his book puts the question, 'But where do the formal similarities actually come from between the sayings of the oriental wandering preachers as sketched by Celsus and the sayings of Jesus in the John Gospel? Did Celsus, or rather did the men whom he met in Palestine, knowingly copy the John Gospel, and use it as an example? Such a solution is completely unlikely'. Even if Lohfink does consider such a solution unlikely, he should not withhold from his readers that Celsus was a man who was writing against the Christians, so that the supposition is very possible that the Celsus accounts of the wandering preachers are really a polemic caricature of the words of Jesus as given in John.

Jesus. On the day of the Dionysos feast the temple wells on Andros and Teos were supposed each year to have given wine instead of water. In Elis three empty vessels were put out in the temple on the evening before the Dionysos feast, and on the next day they were full of wine. The date of the Dionysos feast is the night from the 5th to the 6th of January. That is to say that the date of the old Christian feast of baptism equals Christ's Epiphany; the 6th January has been reckoned for ages past as the day of the wedding in Cana.'[104]

Things are, even in this case, much more complicated than they appear from Bultmann's words. Above all a distinction must be made between the dating of a feast day and the reason for this festival. Since a number of Christian festival have manifestly been deliberately arranged on the dates of heathen festivals in order to supersede them, we will agree with Bultmann that the dating of the miracle of Cana probably has some connection with the date of the feast of Dionysos.

The establishment of this fact says nothing about the general purport of the festival. The fact that the report on the miracle at Cana is older than the dating of these happenings on the 6th January, is something which even Bultmann can hardly dispute.

This can however, be said on the question of a possible transfer of the miracle theme: since there were at that time only two standard drinks, wine and water (apart from milk), and since wine was the noblest and water was the humblest drink, the thought of turning water into wine is so apt that even in a narrative without a historical background there is no need for a transfer of theme from one place to another. For that reason Bultmann's words yield nothing towards the question of the historicity of this event.

The same applies to numerous other references. Under the impression left by the quantity of the material which he has gathered together, Bultmann has neglected to ask critically in every case after the degree of probability with which conclusions may be drawn from this material. Thus for example he does not engage in any reflections on the point that parallel stories by no means depend the one on the other in all cases.

If even such complicated discoveries as porcelain, gun-powder, or infinitesimal calculus were made in various parts of

104 Bulmann, Synoptische Tradition, op. cit., p. 253.

71

the world independent of each other, as we know, then it is simply not a matter of mature reflection to assume that miracle stories, which are similar to each other in the one or the other characteristic, must of necessity be dependent on each other. Since almost all the miracles provide help at times of definite human need, such as death, illness, stormy weather, hunger or thirst, and since these needs are widespread, the dependency of one miracle report on the other can only then be stated if this dependency can be exactly shown or can at least be made to appear probable by means of sound circumstantial indices. A plain reference to a certain parallelism does not say a thing. For this reason nothing has been gained from a scientific point of view by the whole maze of suppositions which Bultmann offers, as long as the material is not critically examined.

6. The last point to which attention is called is that the view put forward by Bultmann as well as Marxsen and others, that 'the taking over of patterns of presentation'[105] can be observed in the biblical accounts of the healing miracles, is both bewildering and meaningless.

Marxsen writes, 'Miracle stories were told at that time about many men, by no means only of Jesus. If one now compares such miracle stories outside the New Testament with each other, then it is noticeable that they are very often told according to a certain fixed pattern. It goes like this: first the severity of the sickness or the suffering is explained, during which it is stressed that many people have already tried to cure this illness or that suffering. Then the meeting with the performer of miracles follows, who brings about the healing. This often happens through intricate manipulations (through touching, by the application of the miracle worker's spittle on the sick limb, also through the recitation of incomprehensible words). As soon as the cure has been effected, its success is at once demonstrated. Lame people walk and throw their crutches away or carry their bed forth. At the end there is then a so-called chorus ending by which those standing around express their astonishment and break forth in praise of the worker of miracles. That is, as has been said, the buildup of such miracle stories outside the New Testament. It is not difficult to recognize though that many of these features are also encountered in the New Testament miracle stories.'[106]

105 Marxsen, op. cit. Introduction, p. 112.     106 id., The Dispute, p. 53 f.

72

This 'pattern' is by its very nature so obvious that it would indeed be astonishing if it were not to be found in countless healing stories, and indeed also in many which are quite independent of each other in a literary sense. The fact that in a healing miracle first the affliction, then the meeting with the performer of miracles, and finally the success are described, is such a factual manner of presentation, that it is almost misleading to talk of a pattern at all. It is even more improper to maintain that this 'pattern' was taken over by the evangelists. The impartial reader of miracle demonstrations notices, especially in the New Testament, that a surprising variety of features deviate from the said 'pattern'. Therefore Marxsen himself concludes his explanations of the miracle pattern, which begins so shakily, with the subdued sentence, 'It is not difficult to recognize though, that many of these features are also encountered in the New Testament miracle stories.'

Why then this high-flown theory about the taking over of traditional patterns? The theory strikes a calm thinking person as grotesquely as if a historian were to call attention, in a declaration on the account of a battle, to the fact that the sequence of the presentation occurs according to a traditional pattern. According to this pattern first the marching up of the troops, then the development of the battle, and finally the result and the losses are to be recounted by way of demonstration. The historian generally prefers to do without such indisputably correct but not very informative references.

## 6. The resurrection as a subject of historical research

The vital event which led to the proclamation of the Gospel, namely the resurrection of Jesus Christ, belongs most certainly to those events which are most in dispute in theology today. Rudolf Bultmann states that 'such a miraculous happening in nature as the vivifying of a dead person'[107] is not worthy of belief. He is convinced 'that a corpse cannot come alive again, and cannot rise out of the grave.'[108]

A preconceived idea is revealed by such a statement, which thereby excludes itself from historical questioning from the very start. Of course no scholar approaches texts without any prejudices at all. In this sense though, a scholar can record his doubts if he comes across information which contradicts his everyday experience. He must not exaggerate this mistrust to such an extent though, that he ties himself down and is therefore not willing to examine the reliability of texts critically, that is to say with the will to accept them or reject them according to the actual state of affairs. He who is determined from the very beginning to declare an account to be unhistorical is, in his way, just as uncritical as a person who considers the same account from the start to be historical.

Apart from that there lies in Bultmann's statement a vital misunderstanding of the accounts of the resurrection themselves. Bultmann talks of a 'miraculous happening in nature'. In the biblical accounts though, the resurrection is not described as a natural event, but as a great deed of God. The difference becomes clear at once if one thinks of the fact that doctors have repeatedly succeeded in calling back to life people who are clinically dead. In the latter case we are not concerned with a 'miraculous happening in nature'. If the doctors had not given impulses to nature, but let

107 Bultmann, Rudolf, Neues Testament und Mythologie. Das Programm der Entmythologisierung der neutestamentlichen Verkündigung, Kerygma und Mythos, Bd. 1, 4 erweiterte Auflage, 1960, p. 29.
108 Jaspers, Karl/Bultmann, Rudolf, Die Frage der Entmythologisierung, München, 1954, p. 51.

74

matters take their course, then these people would have remained dead. Considered purely as natural happenings these great feats of medicine are just not credible. In spite of that no one is in any doubt that the clinically dead have been called back to life.

Of course there was no team of doctors who cared for the dead after Jesus was laid in the tomb. Nevertheless the expression 'miraculous natural happening' misses the point of the problem, for we are not dealing here with the point of whether the vivifying of a dead person is unworthy of belief in the sense of it being a natural event, but with the question of the vivifying of a dead person as a great deed of God.

Arising from those scientific and theoretical reflections which have been considered in dealing with the credibility of the miracles, it follows that there is no reason for excluding the resurrection, right from the start, as a great deed of God. This statement also is especially valid if one bears in mind that the resurrection of Jesus — in comparison with other miracles, and even with other raisings from the dead — possesses a special quality of its own. Those who were healed by Jesus were not immune from fresh illnesses, and those who were raised from the dead died again. It is reported though of Jesus that he rose from the dead and did not die again.

Without going into the additional difficulty which has just been mentioned, it must be stated that the question of the credibility of the New Testament stories must first be approached by historical methods, even on the question of the resurrection. Fortunately Marxsen, as opposed to Bultmann basically accepts the admissability of, and the special right to historical questioning, in that he writes, 'now it is simply not permissible to make our (still limited) experience the measure of what once happened and how it happened ... Such a procedure would be unscientific, because it links two types of method (of history and of science) together in a way which is not permissible.'[109] If the historian asks about Jesus' resurrection, then he is above all concerned with a critical evaluation of the sources. Two facts are reported there: the tomb in which Jesus was laid after he was taken down from the cross was found empty; and Jesus, a living Jesus, appears on a number of occasions to a variable number of people.

109 Marxsen, Willi, Die Auferstehung Jesu von Nazareth, Gütersloh, 1968, p. 24 f.

## (a) *The reports on the appearances of the Risen Christ*

The oldest item of information about the appearance of the Risen Christ appears in the First Letter of Paul the Apostle to the Corinthians. The text in its context reads, 'And now, my brothers, I must remind you of the gospel that I preached to you; the gospel which you received, on which you have taken your stand, and which is now bringing you salvation. Do you still hold fast the Gospel as I preached it to you? If not, your conversion was in vain. First and foremost, I handed on to you the facts which had been imparted to me: that Christ died for our sins, in accordance with the scriptures; that he was buried; that he was raised to life on the third day according to the scriptures; and that he appeared to Cephas, and afterwards to the Twelve. Then he appeared to over five hundred of our brothers at once, most of whom are still alive, though some have died. Then he appeared to James and afterwards to all the apostles. In the end he appeared even to me; though this birth of mine was monstrous . . . Now if this is what we proclaim, that Christ was raised from the dead, how can some of you say that there is no resurrection of the dead? If there be no resurrection, then Christ was not raised; and if Christ was not raised, then our Gospel is null and void, and so is your faith; and we turn out to be lying witnesses for God, because we bore witness that he raised Christ to life, whereas, if the dead are not raised, he did not raise him. For if the dead are not raised, it follows that Christ was not raised; and if Christ was not raised, your faith has nothing in it and you are still in your old state of sin. It follows also that those who have died within Christ's fellowship are utterly lost. If it is for this life only that Christ has given us hope, we of all men are most to be pitied . . . If the dead are never raised to life, 'let us eat and drink, for tomorrow we die.'[110]

This account is remarkable in two respects:

(a) It appears from the account that the question of the resurrection of Jesus Christ had already been recognized at the earliest times as a key question for the Christians, and that the message of the resurrection of Jesus who had died for our sins was actually the Gospel.

(b) The account shows that the resurrection, in the opinion of Paul the Apostle, was an event which — like other events —

110  1. Corinth 15.

needed impeccable witnesses in order to be worthy of belief. For this reason Paul brings forward the evidence of these witnesses. He underlines thereby that most of the witnesses quoted are still living, that is to say are still capable of being questioned.

The First Letter to the Corinthians was in all probability written in Ephesus in the spring of the year 56 or 57, therefore at a time which is very near to the happenings which are testified. The heart of the resurrection testimony, which in the opinion of most of the experts closes with the mention of the Twelve, is still older though. This testimony, or fixed form of words, probably originates from Jerusalem, from where it was 'handed down' to Paul, as he writes. It became a set formula even in the first decade after the crucifixion. Compared with the formula which was handed down and extended in the First Letter to the Corinthians the remaining reports of the appearances of the resurrected Christ were fixed later. In their contents, however, they fully confirm the formula in Corinthians, and also include closer details about various appearances, which to be sure differ from each other not insignificantly, so that Willi Marxsen claims that the reports of the resurrection are historically worthless.

Against such a point of view Erich Stier has rightly remarked, 'As a classical historian I must say this, the sources for the resurrection of Jesus, with their relatively big contradictions over details, present for the historian for this very reason a criterion of extraordinary credibility. For if that were the fabrication of a congregation or of a similar group of people, then the tale would be consistently and obviously complete. For that reason every historian is especially sceptical at that moment when an extraordinary happening is only reported in accounts which are completely free of contradictions.'[111]

A completely unanimous presentation would only then be expected when there existed either a sort of church censorship authority, which had succeeded in forcing through a single official version of the happenings, or if through some misfortune only one single version had remained intact.

Further to this general stipulation the biblical texts do in fact give us a clue as to how the relatively large variations in the resurrection reports arose. It comes to notice at once that the

111 Stier, Hans Erich, Moderne Exegese und historische Wissenschaft, op. cit., p. 152

oldest gospel, the Mark Gospel, does not report on the appearances of the Risen Christ, but — as far as one gathers from the original text — closes with the finding of the empty tomb, whilst the reports of the appearances of the Risen Christ were added only afterwards as a new conclusion to the Mark Gospel.

A comparative study of all available texts leads to the conclusion that the reports of all the appearances of Jesus after Easter were fixed and set down relatively late, later than the accounts of the passion and later than the accounts of the public life and works of Jesus. It does seem at first glance to suggest that the reports of the appearance of the Risen Christ are relatively late 'findings'.

. The collection of evidence, however, stands as a whole in a different light. Almost all commentators are agreed that the Easter happening must be understood as the key event of the whole Christian message. Accordingly even the Gospels as a whole are subject to the impression of the Easter events. That also applies to the Mark Gospel. Although it mentions nothing about the appearances of the Risen Christ, it refers in so many places to the resurrection, so that one can rightly state that the whole conception, even of this gospel, points to the appearance of the Risen Christ.

These words are to be found, 'And he began to teach them that the Son of Man had to undergo great sufferings, and to be rejected by the elders, chief priests, and doctors of the law; to be put to death, and to rise again three days afterwards.'[112] The story of the transfiguration concludes with these words, 'On their way down from the mountain, he enjoined them not to tell anyone what they had seen until the Son of Man had risen from the dead.'[113] And then again, 'he was teaching his disciples, and telling them, 'The Son of Man is now to be given up into the power of men, and they will kill him, and three days after being killed, he will rise again.' But they did not understand what he said, and were afraid to ask.'[114] Or this, 'He took the Twelve aside and began to tell them what was to happen to him. 'We are now going to Jerusalem,' he said; 'and the Son of Man will be given up to the chief priests and the doctors of the law; they will condemn him to death and hand him over to the foreign power. He will be mocked and spat upon, flogged and killed; and three days

112 Mark 8, 31 ff.     113 Mark 9, 9.     114 Mark 9, 31 f.

78

afterwards will rise again.'[115] In a similar way according to the Mark Gospel Jesus declares before his arrest on the Mount of Olives, 'You will all fall from your faith; for it stands written; 'I will strike the shepherd down and the sheep will be scattered. Nevertheless, after I am raised again I will go on before you into Galilee.'[116] Finally Mark reports how the passers-by hurled abuse at Him on the cross, wagging their heads and saying, 'Aha! You would pull the temple down, would you, and build it in three days.'[117]

Thus the following conclusion arises from all this: on the one hand all four gospels are drawn up under the impression left by the Easter happenings; on the other hand the reports on the appearances of the Risen Christ are relatively speaking their latest sections. At first this seems paradoxical. If one keeps in mind though the situation as a whole then it is not nearly so astonishing as it appears at first glance.

The resurrection of Jesus, the triumph of the Lord after the fearful catastrophe of Good Friday, was the key event of the Faith and of the Gospel. It stood out before the eyes of the followers in all its vividness. The immediate witnesses were living, and proclaimed what they had seen and what they had experienced. There were very early on fixed forms of avowal, which had the facts about the death and resurrection of Jesus in their contents, yet no fixed accounts of the appearances of the Risen Christ. This can only be explained in this way, that not a single original report was preserved of what is probably the oldest appearance of the Risen Christ, that is, the appearance to Peter, although the fact itself of this appearance is testified to in essence on a number of occasions, so that there can be no doubt about it historically. Whether the one appearance which is given in the report on the wonderful catch of fish, and reported in the postscript to the John Gospel, was set down later, as Willi Marxsen suspects, will probably never be discovered with absolute certainty.

The whole findings are closely connected with the production of the New Testament writings. As has already been shown, this is a matter of a complete tradition from the very beginning, which is told and transmitted. The finished stories did not cover right from the start the period of time from the birth of Jesus to the final appearance of the Risen Christ. It can be said with a fair

115 Mark 10, 32 f.      116 Mark 14, 27 f.      117 Mark 15, 29.

degree of certainty that the stories of the passion were the crystallization point of the whole tradition. Even Bultmann tends to the view 'that the connection here was the primary one.'[118]

As we can gather from the general conception of the Mark Gospel, a larger framework, which was clearly defined, began to form at an early stage. At first the stories which were fixed orally began with the coming of John the Baptist and the baptism of Jesus. The baptism of Jesus indicates the point in time for the early Christian tradition at which the events around Jesus take on a central importance. That is why there is the demand during the choice of an apostle to take the place of the fallen Judas that this man must have experienced everything at first hand 'beginning with John's baptism'.

Whilst there is almost complete unanimity on the fact that the gospels originally began with Jesus' baptism, there is a general lack of clarity about which happening originally marked the close of the gospels. The termination of the gospels, as they are now in front of us, is remarkably lacking in unanimity. The Matthew Gospel ends with the appearance of Jesus before the eleven disciples in Galilee and the order to baptize men everywhere. The John Gospel ends with the appearance before Thomas, then takes up once again with several stories which carry the tale on, and finally closes with the appearance before Peter and John. Only the Luke Gospel ends with a somewhat brief indication of the ascension. This is reported in more detail in the second book of Luke, namely the Acts of the Apostles. The Mark text which is now available also finally ends with a reference to the ascension. There is, however, unanimity on the point that the last stories have been added subsequently. The genuine Mark text closes with the report of the finding of the empty tomb, and ends with the sentences, 'Then they went out and ran away from the tomb, beside themselves with terror. They said nothing to anybody, for they were afraid.'[119]

Much has been said and written about this piece of evidence. People have generally speaking considered it hard to believe that the Mark Gospel was in fact concluded in this way, and believed that the original ending either got lost or that it was deliberately

118 Bultmann, Rudolf, Synoptische Tradition, op. cit., p. 297.
119 Mark 16, 8.

80

removed since it would have contradicted the later interpretation and conception of the evangelists.[120]

If one seeks to avoid adventurous speculation, and takes the text just as it is, then there are two points which are relevant:

1. As has already been shown, the whole concept of the Mark Gospel leads up to the appearances of the Risen Christ. Jesus foretells in a number of passages that he will die and rise again. In the last chapter of the Mark Gospel it is proclaimed to the women standing before the tomb, 'Fear nothing; you are looking for Jesus of Nazareth who was crucified. He has risen; he is not here; look, there is the place where they laid him. But go and give this message to his disciples and Peter: He will go on before you into Galilee and you will see him there, as he told you.'[121]

2. The Mark Gospel does not include a single report on the appearances of the Risen Christ. Certainly Jesus, according to Mark's report, had predicted many times that he would rise from the dead, and indeed the women do in fact find the tomb empty, and not only that but they again receive the information that he has risen from the dead; yet a confirmation that all those predictions have in fact come to pass is entirely missing from Mark's account.

This dual piece of evidence is there for consideration. The question of an explanation for it was for a long time a matter for dispute. It appears to me that in the meantime a convincing answer has been found. The proclamation of the key message, which is that of the resurrection, was originally reserved for the apostles and those few equals who had themselves experienced the appearances of the Risen Christ. The account of the subsequent choosing of an apostle, which is given in Luke's Acts of the Apostles, taken in conjunction with other passages, shows that apparently not everyone was entitled to report on the resurrection, and that we are concerned here with a strictly limited circle of people who had the duty of being a 'witness to His

120 Such a supposition is simply absurd, because so many references to the resurrection of Jesus are to be found in the Mark text, that it is out of the question that an 'even earlier conclusion' to the Mark text might have contradicted the reports of the other gospels on decisive points.
121 Mark 16, 6 f.

resurrection'. It is for that reason that Paul places so much worth on being in line with those others to whom Jesus had appeared.

Fixed accounts, such as that of the Mark Gospel, originally served the purpose then of leading up to the actual climax. This climax, the proclamation of the resurrection, did not, however, result in the very early period in precise and determined phrases, but always as a free proclamation of those witnesses to the Risen Christ.

This postulation cannot be proved with the last degree of certainty. This can be said for it though, it explains adequately two different facts which at first sight appear unusual. Firstly it becomes clear that the very oldest accounts of the life of Jesus had in fact to be broken off with the finding of the empty tomb, as the proclamation of the resurrection was originally not a matter for the gospel writers, but for the apostles who were witnesses to the Risen Christ. Arising from that is the second point that the accounts of the resurrection did not belong to the early fixed oral tradition, and that they were therefore open in a much stronger way to alteration, and also to the introduction of unhistorical elements. In other words, the astonishingly large differences in the accounts of the appearances of the Risen Christ become completely comprehensible by means of this postulation. The differences are the consequence of the fact that the accounts of the appearances, in contrast to the other parts of the gospels, were not handed on for a long time in a fixed form, but were on each occasion proclaimed in free testimony by the witnesses to the resurrection. They were only added to the Gospel for the first time at a later stage in the handing down. This happened, as far as we can judge from the available texts, for the first time through Luke, that is to say some thirty years after the appearances. Regarding the Easter stories, Marxsen is right that the Evangelists were forced to gather single traditions and string them together.

In view of this situation it is hardly possible to declare certain details of the stories of His appearance to be historically genuine and others to be historically not genuine. The question of the historical genuineness of almost all questions of detail has rather to remain open, provided that one applies the strict criteria of scientific evidence. And there we come to the crux of the matter, 'What part of the reports on the appearances can be considered historically assured?'

82

The first and most important point is this, that the appearances did actually take place. The size and the kind of the circle of witnesses excludes the thought that it is a case of a kind of hallucination which has arisen from lively imaginations. We can conceive even less of a kind of plot by like-minded people, because such a plot would be against the personal interest of those taking part.

According to the reports given in the gospels there can hardly be any doubt that the apostles had fully abandoned the case Jesus after the catastrophe of Good Friday and after the radical swing round of mood in Jerusalem. Only the appearances of Jesus caused a new change of mood. Those who were affected by these appearances confess themselves at last irrevocably to be followers of Jesus, of Him who was crucified as a criminal; and thus they lay themselves open from a worldly point of view to a complete lack of security and to the utmost danger. In fact most of them were killed for this testimony. Erich Stier quite rightly stressed during the course of the aforementioned symposium 'Something must really have taken place here; one cannot simply explain it by saying, 'The impression which Jesus had left behind him in these simple men did not leave them any peace until they thought that they had found the redeeming word for that which they could not understand. Thereby they obtained the power to achieve an unparalleled world-wide effect.' It is asking too much to have to believe something like that. That is just not on. I want to state quite categorically that something like that is historically out of the question. One cannot just switch off all historical experience in this case, simply because it does not suit us to accept that something very tremendous and great must have taken place here.'[122]

On the question of the manner of the appearances we have to consider first, in my opinion, whether all the appearances which are enumerated in the Letter to the Corinthians have the same structure. The possibility of a variation in structure seems to me to have been too little weighed in the balance in the theological discussion. Although Paul puts himself last of those to whom Jesus appeared, I think that the appearance before Paul himself takes a special place from the point of view of its structure. That is shown by the fact that the appearance is only perceived by Paul,

122 Stier, op. cit. p. 152.

and not in the full sense of the word by those who accompanied him. There is a certain similarity in this to the report of the stoning of Stephan. Stephan also sees the majesty of God and Jesus on the right hand of God, without the others perceiving the same thing.

A difference between the appearance before Paul — and in a similar manner before Stephan — and the other appearances which occurred after Easter, must be weighed up all the more carefully as the same reporter — namely Luke — gives an account of both appearances and works out significant differences. They are confirmed by the fact that on the one hand the testimony which Paul himself gives in his letters corresponds with the appropriate account in Luke, and on the other hand the accounts of the other three gospels coincide in their structure with that which Luke tells in his account of the appearance of Jesus within the '40 days'.

Without being drawn in at this point into the theological discussion about the 40 days, one must keep firmly in mind that the meetings after Easter, according to the accounts in the New Testament, carry a special character compared with later appearances, and that these meetings are limited to a definite period. It is noticeable that the disciples after a certain time still expect the Second Coming in Majesty, but yet no further manifest appearances.

Against this whole explanation the point can be raised that in the Letter to the Corinthians Paul records the appearance which he himself witnessed in the list with the after-Easter appearances to the Apostles and the disciples, in that he writes, 'In the end he appeared even to me; though this birth of mine was monstrous.'[123] Paul does not go into the manner of the appearance in any way at this point. Only the fact of the appearance and not the manner is stated.

Anyone who has examined these questions closely knows that Paul had to put up a real struggle to be acknowledged as an apostle. This motive without doubt contributed to the fact that Paul places himself in the Letter to the Corinthians in the same category as the original apostles. Nevertheless this enumeration, in its significance, seems to me to be in no way unequivocal

123  1. Corinth 15, 8.

84

enough to take away the force of the very important arguments which speak against a full identification of the after-Easter appearances with the appearance before Paul. Only this is identical, that Jesus appeared as a living person; and he did that in the sense of an objective notification, which — to speak with the voice of Marxsen — rejects an *extra nos*.

In contrast to the appearance of Jesus before Paul, the peculiarity of the actual Easter appearances lies in the fact that the apostles not only see the Risen Christ but actually associate with Him. Thus there is mention on a number of occasions of a meal shared with the Risen Christ. One tended formerly to the view that these reports were written with the intention of demonstrating the incarnation of the Risen Christ and therefore greeted them with much scepticism; in more recent times however it has quite rightly been pointed out that the accounts of the mutual participation at the meal originally probably had no vindicatory intent, but had a much more immediate and deeper sense; which is illuminating, especially for the historian who always tries to keep in mind the whole context of events.

After Jesus' failure, and after his capture and the radical swing round of the general mood in Jerusalem, the disciples, afraid and perplexed, gave up everything. Jesus dies on the cross, surrounded by his enemies, forsaken by his disciples.

The communion which reached a fresh climax at the last supper was radically broken up by the human failure of the apostles. The Risen Christ appears to those apostles. His appearance apparently not only means a pleasant surprise to those concerned, but also a painful embarrassment. It is not only a matter of Him who was crucified by his enemies, but also the master who was forsaken by the very apostles themselves, who was in part denied and betrayed. It is He who appears there. Yet he speaks the words of peace, and documents his attitude in that he breaks bread with them as in former times. The most intimate community as known from olden times, namely the common supper, was restored.

If one bears in mind this context, then the accounts of the meal shared with the Risen Christ cannot just be written off from the start as tendentious accounts to demonstrate the incarnation of the Risen Christ. It should moreover always be kept in mind that the very same reports also make public the special charac-

85

teristics of the risen body. He is able to go through closed doors and to disappear before their eyes.

The question of the incarnation of the Risen Christ leads directly to the second fact which is stated in the New Testament — to the empty tomb.

### (b)  *The testimony of the empty tomb*

All four evangelists report on the finding of the empty tomb. In addition to the testimonies of the Gospels there is, in my opinion, the independent witness of two sermons within the Acts of the Apostles.

In Peter's Pentecost sermon are to be found these words, 'Let me tell you plainly, my friends, that the patriarch David died and was buried, and his tomb is here to this very day. It is clear therefore that he spoke as a prophet . . . when he said he was not abandoned to Hades, and his flesh never suffered corruption.'[124] This sermon by Peter is parallel to the Paul sermon in Antioch, which is also recorded in the Acts of the Apostles. It is so recorded, 'As for David, when he had served the purpose of God, he died, and was gathered to his fathers, and suffered corruption; but the one whom God raised up did not suffer corruption.'[125]

These passages are especially significant, as the empty tomb of Jesus is not specifically mentioned, and yet is assumed to be known, in that it is put forward as a contrast to the tomb in which the Patriarch David suffered mortification. The fact that Luke brings this sermon out in two different passages, and attributes it to two different preachers, tends towards the conclusion that he was dealing here with a standard topic of the mission to the Jews which was widely known. The question as to who brought in the contrast between David and Jesus with reference to the tomb must remain open. There can be no doubt about it that this sermon pattern is very old. It is one of the oldest testimonies handed down to us about the empty tomb.

It is maintained by quite a number of theologians that Paul may not have known anything about the empty tomb. The only point about that which is correct is that Paul does not mention the tomb specifically in any passage, for the Paul sermon in Antioch which has just been quoted from the Acts of the Apostles,

124 Acts 2, 29 ff.    125 Acts 13, 36 ff.

86

obviously cannot be evaluated as an authentic testimony of Paul's. On the other hand it appears from the statements in the Letter to the Corinthians that Paul knew about this tomb. The formulation which he uses not only gives the message of the death and resurrection of Jesus, but also speaks specifically of the laying to rest in the tomb, which took place between these two events. The four past participles used in the Paul formulation are dead, buried, risen, and appeared. It can hardly be assumed that the past participles 'risen' and 'appeared' are both in antithesis only to 'dead'. The philological analysis rather shows an ingenious sentence structure which has certainly not come about by chance. Each of the key declarations which are in antithesis, 'dead' and 'risen', are underlined by the additional phrase 'according to the scriptures'. And each of these declarations which are in antithesis has been complemented by a statement rounding off the declaration concerned. It would be an outrageous interpretation in my opinion if one removed one of these past participles from the antithetical structure of the whole phrase. The declaration 'dead and buried according to the scriptures' stands in antithesis and parallel to the declaration 'risen and appeared again according to the scriptures'. This sentence construction leads to the conclusion that, according to the formulation used by Paul, the two facts 'dead and buried' are emphasized by the two facts 'rose and appeared again'. That means though that this old formulation includes the fact of the empty tomb.

To all this must be added the fact that the Jews did not know the idea of a purely spiritual life after death. Everyone who maintained that Jesus had risen from the dead had to reckon accordingly with the possibility that this statement would be checked by an examination of the tomb.

With this in mind Wolfgang Pannenberg correctly writes, 'Let us imagine just how the disciples in Jerusalem were in a position to announce His waking from the dead if they could be constantly contradicted by the observation of the tomb in which the body of Jesus had been laid'. T. Althaus has rightly seen the point here that 'In Jerusalem, at the place where Jesus was put to death, and at the tomb, it is announced not long after His death that he has woken from the dead. This fact demands that they had a reliable witness in the circle of the first group of followers that the tomb was found empty.' The Christian teaching (kerygma) of the rising again 'could not have been maintained for a single day in Jerusalem, let alone for a single hour, if the emptiness of the tomb had not been accepted as a fact by all those taking part.'[126]

In fact they are all apparently in agreement on the factuality of the empty tomb. Jewish polemics began at once against the preaching of the resurrection. There is no Jewish polemic however against the claim that the tomb is empty. The whole of the Jewish polemics, just like the preaching of the Christian Gospel, emanates from the fact of the empty tomb. It is indeed not unanimous in the manner of its presentation. The two most important ways of presentation are:

(a) The disciples got rid of the body,
(b) The gardener first of all removed the dead body to safety in anticipation of the coming deception on the part of the disciples, so that he could later bring it back to the same place and thus reveal the whole swindle of the resurrection.

Hans Freiherr von Campenhausen rightly states that these stories which are in parts quite fantastic, 'nowhere create the impression that they go back to positive observations and genuine old items of news.'[127] They are rather an emergency construction designed to deal with an indisputable and unpleasant fact.

Against these arguments it is a mere supposition, from the point of view of historical scholarship, that an inscription which was found in Nazareth is connected with the fact of the empty tomb. It is rather concerned with the abbreviated repetition of an imperial edict against the stealing of corpses and the desecration of graves.[128] Since decrees were issued or reissued in a sharper form to meet given situations, in those days just as they are now, it has been surmised that in this particular decree a reaction on the part of Emperor Tiberius can be perceived to the reports of the

126 Pannenberg, Wolfhart, Die historische Problematik der Auferstehung Jesu, Grundzüge der Christologie, Gütersloh, 1964, p. 97 f.
127 Campenhausen, Hans Freiherr von, Der Ablauf der Osterereignisse und das leere Grab, Sitzungsbericht der Heidelberger Akademie der Wissenschaften, Heidelberg, Second Edition 1958, p. 52.
128 cf. Stauffer, E., Jesus, Dalp 332, p. 11. Also literature.

Governor Pontius Pilate to the killing of Jesus, and the subsequent events.

The historian would grant that Pontius Pilate very likely gave a report to Rome of the crucifixion of Jesus and the relevant happenings, since in the prevailing situation, after the overthrow and execution of his protector Sejan, it must have suited him that the matters should be made known in Rome, to an always distrustful emperor, in a version which put him in a favourable light. The historian will moreover grant that Pilate's report could very possibly be the reason for the imperial decree, or alternatively for the increased severity. But those are pure speculations. According to the present state of historical research it cannot be shown with the necessary degree of certainty that there is a connection between the inscription at Nazareth and the finding of the empty tomb.

As clearly as all the relevant sources either specifically testify to the empty tomb, or assume it to be a fact, so do they vary just as strongly from each other in the details of presentation. Mention has already been made of the Jewish polemics, which claim to know about the theft of the corpse by the disciples, or about some action on the part of the gardener. Yet even the gospels display variations in detail. As has already been shown though, this kind of difference does not affect the reliability of the sources with regard to the key testimony. After full consideration, and the assessment of all the sources in mind, the following points seem to meet the historical circumstances.

1. The discovery of the empty tomb is first made apparently by women who are from the followers of Jesus. Even though women were not legally entitled at that time to bear witness, it is unlikely that this information was found to be in contradiction of the facts. Very probably the details given by the women were checked at a later date by members of the group of apostles. Confirmation comes not only from the fact that the information is found in several gospels, but even more so from the point that from its very nature it is more than likely that in those days a report given by women would be checked by men.

2. Apparently the shroud and the linen cloths aroused special attention at the time of the discovery at the tomb. An interpretation of the appropriate passages is given in the careful textual analysis which Eberhard G. Auer has put forward in his

enquiry on 'The Third Day'.[129] The basic findings of Auer concerning the linen cloths seem to me to be convincing.

It does not seem reasonable to attribute Luke's announcement, 'Peter, however, got up and ran to the tomb, and peering in, saw the wrappings and nothing more; and he went home amazed at what had happened'[130] to the appropriate passages in John.[131] I consider it much more likely that the compiler of the John Gospel wanted to improve the Luke text by means of additions, as he did in a number of other passages. The description of the so-called 'race by the disciples to the tomb', which already leads to the linen cloths and the detailed description of the bands and the cloth, can hardly be explained unless one assumes a very definite historical background.

The story of the guards which is told in the Matthew Gospel must also be taken into consideration. In the form in which it is told by Matthew this story of the guards is scarcely credible from a historical point of view. On the other hand it is just too easy to assume that Matthew simply thought this story up to confront the Jewish account of the theft of the body. According to our experience, things are usually not as simple as that in secular history. It must rather be assumed that the account of the guard at the tomb, as given by Matthew, arose as the result of some actual happening or other. In my opinion it happened according to the practice which is typical of the appropriate officials at all times and in all places, that the authorities in Jerusalem undertook a search immediately the fact of the empty tomb became known, shut off the scene of this unusual happening for the time being, and sealed it up. This applies especially in a case where there are traces of some unusual occurrence in the tomb itself, as Auer convincingly shows. If Jesus' tomb was in fact temporarily sealed and watched by Jewish or Roman officials after the resurrection, then a sufficient explanation is thereby given of how the guards' story in Matthew could come about. Matthew heard about the guarding of the tomb according to the real recollection of witnesses, probably witnesses at second hand,

129 Auer, Eberhard G., Der dritte Tag — Die Ereignisse nach den Auferstehungsakten der Evangelien. In spite of several differences in detail Auer's main theme seems to be worthy of close attention.
130 Luke 24, 12.
131 John 20, 3 ff.

and included this item of information in his own report — doubtless with vindicatory intent. Of course that is only a hypothesis. There is much to be said for it, though, because it explains the text of those sources which are actually available, without the bold speculations and lines of thought which are to be found in theological literature.

The finding of the linen sheet and the linen cloths in the tomb, as reported by Luke and John respectively, leads on to the question of the Turin Shroud, which must be viewed as a unique document of the suffering, the death, and the burial of Jesus, provided that it can finally be considered genuine. The genuineness of the cloth is the subject of considerable controversy though. A few years ago it seemed that only a most credulous person would support that view. The fact that the cloth can only be accounted for from the fourteenth century aroused mistrust. There are, however, enough examples that valuable articles are considered as lost for hundreds of years, and then suddenly reappear. In this respect attention only needs to be drawn to the fate of a number of works of art.

The fact that this concerns a negative imprint which can be dated back to the time of Jesus speaks for the genuineness of the Turin Shroud. A deliberate faking is thereby excluded. Also reference to the fact that the dead person who was wrapped in the cloth need not necessarily have been Jesus of Nazareth, as crucifixion was a frequent and widespread punishment at that time, has little meaning. For the traces of the stigmata, including the crown of thorns, the traces of the lash, and of the spear thrust, are so identical with the story of Jesus' passion, that a chance correspondence is unlikely. Moreover, those who were crucified in those days were not generally granted an honourable burial. And even if one assumes that it happened now and again, there arises the further question as to why anyone unwrapped the dead body after a few days and did not leave it in the tomb.

In view of all this evidence one must say with the greatest reservation that, so far, there is no relatively plausible explanation for the Turin Shroud, unless it is that one accepts its genuineness. If the cloth is indeed genuine, then this means a further confirmation of the historical reliability of the reports in the gospels, as this cloth mirrors the story of Jesus' suffering in all its details. Moreover it is, unless one agrees to the thesis of the

91

theft of the body, an indirect indication of the resurrection, as the cloth would otherwise have remained in the tomb with the dead body.

3. The appearances after Easter found a somewhat conditional conclusion. Independently of the details which are found in the accounts of the ascension, it can be firmly stated that the followers of Jesus, from a certain time onwards, apparently only expect a final Second Coming in Majesty, and on the other hand no longer expect manifest appearances of the Risen Christ.

Even if one accepts, in the light of the whole of the historical evidence, the empty tomb and the appearances of the Risen Christ as historical facts, the related theological problems are no more solved than they are in the case of the miracles. Thus the question, in particular, as to whether Jesus is shown to be the Son of God through the resurrection is not to be explained by means of historical scholarship.

### (c) *Willi Marxsen's Theses on the Resurrection. An Excursus*

The credibility of sources on the resurrection of Jesus is impressively confirmed, not least by the fact that, up to the present day, not one single person has succeeded in giving a convincing interpretation of the sources without accepting the resurrection as a historical event.

Naturally it is not possible to go into the voluminous literature as a whole, but instead the most important of those put forward by Willi Marxsen will be critically examined. As we have already remarked, Marxsen is of the opinion that the reports on the resurrection are historically worthless. He must, however, for his part then give an explanation as to how the sources and reports arose at all. The final result of his comprehensive deliberations are explained by Marxsen himself in this way:

'With that we should have reached a historically fairly certain conclusion. I will try to express it in the most precise way possible. After Good Friday Simon was the first who came to believe in Jesus. We should not express it though as a historical happening that Simon was the first who saw Jesus, but we have to express the connection between believing and seeing thus, that Simon was the first who came to believe. The proof of this 'having come to believe' is that we say that Simon saw Jesus.'[132]

This coming-to-believe on the part of Peter occurred in Galilee, according to Marxsen, perhaps whilst fishing. The content of the believing was the conviction, 'that God confirmed that Jesus was the one, just as he was there. Jesus promised to mankind in his earthly life the forgiveness of sins in the name of God. He demanded of them to direct their life entirely to God, and to let the care for the morrow really be the care for the next day. He demanded of them to be wholly there for their neighbour. He demanded of them to put their life at risk (and that means their attempt to remain firm in their faith). He also demanded of them to stand up for peace where it is dangerous to do so (calculated from a human point of view), because that can mean the abnegation of a person's own rights. And he promised mankind that in the doing of this unreasonable demand they would find the true life, life with God.'[133] 'That means, reduced to a precise phrase, that in the sense of Peter's 'coming-to-believe', Easter means that 'the cause of Jesus' goes on.'[134] According to Marxsen nothing more remains to be said. For 'how Peter experienced it, we can no longer say with certainty.'[135]

Peter's 'coming to believe' is, then, according to Marxsen, the reason for all Christian believing. He underlines it, 'By that, Peter is now really the rock of the Church. It is immaterial how his faith was induced.'[136] Thereupon Marxsen continues logically, 'Why is it told that the individual groups witnessed an appearance of Jesus? what do we mean by that? I think that their faith, and the manifold functions which they carried out, are all finally based on the first appearance before Peter. They are all included in this first appearance.'[137] 'Then a group was formed which carried on the mission; Peter, some of the Twelve, and others. Those were the Apostles. Now we will answer the question on what foundation they carried on the mission. And as reason is named the point that they have seen Jesus.'[138] This statement according to Marxsen should not be understood though as a historical statement. 'The followers who came to the faith after Good

---

132 Marxsen, Die Auferstehung, op. cit. p. 99.
133 id. p. 127 f.        134 id. p. 129 etc.
135 id. p. 129.          136 id. p. 129.
137 id. p. 95.           138 id. p. 97.

Friday have realized who Jesus was; and now they also see him thus. They demonstrate a reality, but naturally not a historical one.'[139] 'The picture which we have of the earthly Jesus yields the material with the help of which we visualize the 'having-come-to-believe' after Good Friday. Thus the impression arises that the life of Jesus still goes on a little bit on this earth. The 'Earthly One' meets the disciples after his death, speaks with them, sends them out.' 'Existing functions (however they may have arisen) are founded on a 'having seen' which had its origin in the first 'having seen' by Peter.'[140]

The news of the resurrection, according to Marxsen's convictions, is correspondingly not concerned with historical facts. Resurrection, raising up, and the empty tomb are, rather, interpretaments which serve to make the 'having come to believe' intelligible to others. 'We learn in a wonderful manner that Jesus goes on in the faith after his death. Now we ask after the reason which makes this 'coming-to-believe' possible. The reason is — the dead Jesus lives. He did not therefore stay dead. Now if we wanted to describe a dead person as a living one, then the conception of the resurrection of the dead was available. So this was used.'[141]

In place of the interpretaments of the resurrection we could just as well use the interpretament of the raising up, or the interpretament of the empty tomb, in Marxsen's view, in order to express the idea that the cause of Jesus lives on. It is only in the later development of the Tradition, above all through Luke's work, that the various interpretaments are so welded together that they come apparently to be misunderstood by a modern person as reports on historical happenings.

Against these ideas of Marxsen it has been put forward by the church that the conclusions show that Marxsen has fallen into theological error. Marxsen for his part turned with passionate vehemence against this kind of rejoinder, in that he wrote, 'If one really wishes to refute my conclusions, then one must show where I have made a mistake on the way towards my conclusions.'[142]

This manner of arguing by Marxsen is of course unrealistic. It accords with our daily experience that we sometimes come first to the conclusion that we have made a mistake at some point or

139 id. p. 163.    140 id. p. 108.
141 id. p. 141.    142 id. p. 142.

94

other, without being clear for the moment where the mistake lies. Our children experience this already at school. It often happens that they come home after doing work in class and tell us that in this or that exercise they reached a result which was surely wrong; yet they do not know where they have miscalculated. Many car drivers experience the same thing. They suddenly find out that they have lost their way without being in a position to say at what crossroads or fork they took the wrong turning. Simply from the result it can of necessity be concluded that an error has occurred.

The point arises from all this that it is not actually inadmissible to conclude from the result that something has been done wrongly. The only thing that Marxsen can demand is the demonstration that the result cannot in fact be correct. As a non-theologian I do not feel myself called upon to decide whether Marxsen's conclusion can be shown to be false within the meaning of theological scholarship. For that reason I wish to confine myself to the historical aspect.

Is it credible historically that Peter came to believe in Galilee whilst fishing, in a manner about which nothing more specific can be said, and that then this coming-to-believe of Peter's spread to others, that these then began to carry out the Mission, and that they finally had to seek a justification of their doings and to proclaim in justification, 'We have seen Jesus'? Whereby then this having seen Jesus, which in its turn means nothing more than the having-come-to-believe, could be expressed in a different way, either in the precise wording that Jesus rose from the dead, or in the precise wording that the tomb was found, or again in the precise wording that Jesus is risen? Is this credible historically?

And is it credible historically that these different interpretaments then very quickly made themselves self-evident more or less in such a way that they were handed down by all compilers of New Testament writings in a form which led people astray, who had not yet been taught better by Marxsen, and who took them up as reports of an historical event?

The historian can only answer these questions in the negative, and will recall thereby a saying of the Dutch historian, Johan Huizinga, who on one occasion wrote, 'Even the most hypercritical historian, the sceptic to the highest degree, is forced to take refuge in fanciful constructions for his divergent presentation of the facts, whereby he falls from his critical doubt into bottomless gullibility.'[143] It is quite fanciful and incredible that the sources — as we possess them and can at any time check them — were ever formulated in that way, should Marxsen's reconstruction have hit upon reality.

Now it can be said with a certain justification that even if we can conclude from the result that there is a mistaken effort, then we must be able to determine by precise research the exact spot at which a mistake was made. Even the pupil, who first notices that the solution to his task cannot be right as it is, has a right to learn what he has done wrong in detail. Many car drivers who have lost their way, are not satisfied with the establishment of the fact that they are off route, but they check from the map the place at which they chose the wrong road. We generally like to know not only that we have done something wrong but also how the mistake came about. Likewise one can demand that this investigation is not complete with a demonstration that Marxsen has arrived at false conclusions, but it must also show where mistakes in his reflections lie. This task is indeed not so easy to carry out as it first appears. For Marxsen is like a driver who loses the way in sweeping arcs and detours. He does not arrive at his remarkable conclusion by making a striking mistake at one spot in his train of thought, but through the fact that he systematically pushes in one particular direction in lengthy hypothetical reflections. It is characteristic of his way of working that he complains that we have unfortunately 'almost always asked questions too directly'.[144] We are certainly forced to admit that a long and careful process is often rewarding in scholarship, and that roundabout ways of thinking have now and again led to good results. At the same time we have to beware of the dangers which lie in a multitude of single very small steps. The room for error which lies in every single hypothesis, taken with the room for error in the following hypotheses, can add up, so that the end result is no longer worth discussing.

In view of this situation I will content myself with demonstrating by a number of points and by way of example Marxsen's arbitrary line of thought.

1. Even Marxsen asks himself the question how it came that

143 Huizinga, Johan, Im Banne der Geschichte, Zürich, Second Edition 1942 p. 70.

144 Marxsen, Die Auferstehung, op. cit. p. 102.

Peter's having-come-to-believe and that of the apostles was presented as an issue from the Easter happenings. He declares, 'According to many of the previous expositions one might be inclined to answer that already at an early date the presentation (the resurrection of Jesus), with the help of which the reality of the having-come-to-believe was expressed, was separated from this reality, and then this presentation was built up on its own. But that would not meet the case. It is necessary to know that whereas we use conceptions, the ancients, especially orientals, often expressed themselves in pictures. I will make that clear with a play on words which is very near to our problem. Where we perceive something, they see something. A train of thought which we develop abstractly, they often represent as having been seen. What we think of together often appears in their case in sequence. At this point we are very likely to make mistakes when we want to understand the old manner of presentation. That is connected with the fact that we who are living in the tradition of the Aufklärung have learnt to distinguish between what really happened and what that which has happened can say, what it causes, what it means, and so on. For us, both are separate, the one from the other; and if we come across such presentations we automatically separate them. Then we judge historically. We say that this or that did not happen at all in the way in which it is represented. We are certainly right in this judgement. Only we easily overlook that this judgement is anachronistic; for we bring a differentiation to bear which was still foreign to the compiler.'[145]

Anyone who has ever concerned himself with the history of ideas knows though that the idea of an absolute division, namely before and after the Aufklärung, which is here put forward by Marxsen, is a false one. At the latest since the birth of philosophical thinking in classical times there has permanently been an enlightenment (Aufklärung) in the history of European ideas, and since the founding of historical writing by Herodotus and Thucydides, the question has been asked again and again whether events handed down are to be seen historically and whether they took place in detail in the way in which they are reported. In so far as sagas and myths found their way into historical works, at this higher stage of reflection they were specifically marked as such, and in this way dropped from history.

145 id. p. 159 f.

Instead of many examples, one sentence from the beginning of Livy is worth quoting, 'One accepts of olden times that they make the founding of cities more noble in that they let the human and the godly act in unison.'[146]

A similarly critical attitude is to be found way back in mediaeval history. Thus for example Otto von Freising writes in his chronicle of the known world, 'Furthermore the noble archbishop Thiemo was taken prisoner, and as is reported, he was forced to hold a service to a false diety. However he asked for time to think, went into the temple, and being extraordinarily strong in the powers of soul and body, he smashed the idols to pieces which he should pray to. He thereby proved that they were no gods but the work of man. He was therefore brought before the court and crowned with a glorious martyrdom, suffering under specially chosen torments and tortures of all kinds. That he suffered this because of his Christian faith is a completely reliable tradition; that he smashed the idols is already hard to believe because it is well-known that all the Saracens only worship one God.'[147] Even here the question of the historical proceedings and the historical credibility is raised, independent of the significance of the story.

Marxsen is doubtless right that questioning was deepened as a result of the Aufklärung and become a general property of a relatively broad layer of learned men. This fact cannot however disguise the point that there was an Aufklärung, an enlightenment, from the sixth century before Christ at the latest, in the whole area of western culture, to which the provinces of the Roman Empire belonged. There are, moreover, still people today who have not yet mentally reached the stage of enlightenment.

It is therefore false when Marxsen presupposes a way of thinking, which is not yet reflective, for all writings which were compiled before the Aufklärung, and when he believes that their compilers collectively and individually did not know how to differentiate between the 'what really happened' and 'what "that which has happened" can say, what it causes, what it means, and so on.' The stage of reflection in which writings are found must, contrary to Marxsen's opinion, always be checked from the writings themselves.

146 Livius, Titus, Ab urbe condita.
147 Freising, Otto von, Chronik VII, 7.

Such an examination is relatively simple in the case of New Testament writings. Their level of reflection is already shown in that parables are almost throughout characterized as parables. It is clearly said, 'He told them yet another parable ...' or 'the Kingdom of Heaven is like a king ...'. The words do not read, 'Jesus said, "Once upon a time there was a king, who held a marriage feast...".' That means that the gospels have a stage of reflective thought in which invented tales are made to stand out against actual details.[148]

On the contrary, in certain cases the assurance is specifically affirmed concerning actual events, that they did indeed come to pass in the manner described. That can happen in differing forms, either the witnesses are named, or by stressing, as in 'He is truly risen', and similar ways. The question whether it is a matter of an actual happening, or not, does not remain open and without reflection, but is decided this way or that.

This analysis shows that it is simply not true when Marxsen maintains that the differentiation between historically factual happenings and the interpretaments of the compilers of the New Testament 'were still unknown'.

The reaction of the Jews and the vindicatory tendencies of the evangelists speak plainly against Marxsen. If Marxsen's lines of thought were indeed correct, then the contemporaries of Jesus, who were certainly living before the time of the Aufklärung, would have radically misunderstood Peter and the

148  Unfortunately there are exegetists who draw an analogy from the Old to the New Testament far too quickly. This is only possible though with the greatest circumspection, for the degree of reflection on the part of the authors of the New Testament is significantly higher with regard to historicity than the majority of the authors of the Old Testament. In fact, in the Old Testament various narrative forms are strung together without reflection, whereas the authors of the New Testament generally indicate quite clearly by direct or indirect references the point at which they include teaching stories within the whole presentation. In other places they specifically stress that certain things have indeed been added, in this way or that. It must also be taken into account that in the historical passages of the Old Testament the distance in time between the happenings and the writing down is generally much greater than in the New Testament. In view of these differences it is misleading when Gerhard Lohfink, in his book 'Jetzt verstehe ich die Bibel' simply strings together examples out of the Old Testament and the New Testament uncritically.

Apostles. The whole quarrel between the Jews and Jesus' disciples would have been completely superfluous. For the point that the disciples had come to believe and that the cause of Jesus was carried on, was not the main point of the quarrel between both sides. The quarrel was rather about whether Jesus really rose from the dead and whether he be the Son of God.

2. Marxsen endeavours to place the news of the empty tomb as an interpretament, which is at first independent, next to the message of the appearances of the Risen Christ. He writes, 'As opposed to the examples already named the stories of the empty tomb form a special case. We saw that Mark offers the oldest attainable form . . . We must pay attention to the fact that the story is self-contained. It does not demand a continuation, which might more or less demand that the Risen Christ must now be seen. We gain this impression only through the fact that we know the later gospels.'[149]

This statement of Marxsen's is itself not correct if — as Marxsen claims — the words of the angel, 'He will go on before you into Galilee and you will see him there, as he told you'[150] did not originally belong to the text. For even the Mark gospel, which in its original state reports nothing about the appearances of the Risen Christ, refers unmistakably in so many places to the resurrection, as we have already explained in some detail in a different connection, so that we must conclude that the whole conception of this gospel also leads up to the appearances of the Risen Christ.

Of course we must ask to what extent some of these formulations were influenced by the later course of events. Of course there are exegetists who are of the opinion, for example, that the story of the transfiguration may well be an anticipated story of the resurrection. Yet in that case especially is Marxsen's opinion absurd, that the report of the finding of the empty tomb is a matter of an interpretament which stands self-contained and of equal importance next to the message of the Risen Christ.

Naturally we can raise an objection and say that Marxsen is referring back to a tradition before Mark. Yet this referring back is not really a back reference, but mere speculation. It is not acceptable from the point of view of scholarship to invent a

149 Marxsen, Die Auferstehung, op. cit. p. 164 f.
150 Mark 16, 7.

pre-Mark tradition by bundling together self-determined hypotheses in order to justify by their exposition risky theories which are contrary to the texts which are actually available.

As much as I tend to the opinion that the discovery of the empty tomb happened before the appearances of the Risen Christ, so little do I find in the available texts any reference to the point that there was a tradition in the early Christian community of the empty tomb without any connection to the resurrection and to the appearances of the Risen Christ.

3. In a number of places Marxsen writes sentences which — as they stand — are just not correct. Here are two examples.

(a) He maintains, 'A seeing is claimed only by those who believe. It is not possible to isolate the seeing from the reality of believing.'[151] We cannot accept the second sentence, that we cannot isolate seeing from believing. The first sentence, that a seeing is only claimed by such as believe, is surely false. For it is expressedly stated after several appearances that first came the seeing, and that the believing followed. The classic example is in Thomas, with whom this sequence becomes plainly thematic. The same applies to Paul. It is just not so that no one saw Jesus who did not believe, but it is just the reverse. The New Testament does not tell of anyone who saw the Risen Christ not coming to believe.

(b) Marxsen writes, 'We must ask namely how Paul brings his Damascus experience into relationship with the statement about the resurrection of Jesus. That occurs significantly only in Corinthians 15.'[152] After this statement there follows a whole load of interpretations, until he closes with, 'Paul lets it nowhere be known that what happened to him before Damascus brought the conviction that Jesus has risen.'[153] 1. Corinthians 15 has then fallen victim to this interpretation!

4. In many places Marxsen gives — without in point of fact saying anything false — a misleading presentation of facts. Here is an example of this:

With reference to a passage in the Letter to the Galatians Marxsen writes, 'If Paul speaks of his Damascus experience, then he must not do it with the word 'see'. He can identify it by another term which has a general meaning such as 'reveal that which was otherwise, or formerly, hidden'. How this disclosure happens is

151 Marxsen, op. cit. p. 143.
152 id. p. 103.     153 id. p. 109.

101

thus left completely open.'[154] Marxsen thus acknowledges that Paul in his Letter to the Corinthians (9, 1 f.) unmistakably calls his Damascus experience a seeing. Marxsen even repeats, 'One thing only is certain, that Paul must not call his experience a seeing.'[155] Finally he declares, 'Thus one can at least suppose that Paul formerly characterized his experience unthinkingly in general as a revelation. The precise wording of this revelation as a seeing then happened for the first time in assimilation to the (probable) customary manner of speech.'[156]

Of course Marxsen can suppose that. But the manner in which he brings this supposition into play leads to error in so far as the degree of probability is played up. It is nevertheless valid to think of the following point. The verb used in the Galatians Letter is more all-inclusive than the verb 'to see'. That means that this verb does not signify a seeing in every case, but it can be used in the sense of seeing. Therefore Marxsen's statement, that Paul must not characterize his experience as a seeing, is meaningless. Of course we can use a comprehensive verb instead of the word 'seeing' in every sentence in which the verb 'to see' appears, such as 'to perceive' or 'to notice'. Now if someone says, about the same event, on the one occasion 'I noticed it' and on the other occasion 'I saw it', then it is meaningless to state that it is certain that the person concerned must not describe this experience as seeing.

To support his thesis Marxsen adds, 'In any case though, an ever bigger approximation to the formulations of the Tradition is to be recognized in the succession of Paul's formulations.'[157] Even this sentence is meaningless, indeed misleading, if we think that the Letter to the Galatians and the First Letter to the Corinthians were written roughly at the same time, so that it cannot even be determined with certainty which of the two is the older. Moreover it must also be considered that the sequence which Marxsen has brought into play can only be assumed to have a fifty-fifty chance according to the rule of probability.

Now indeed a defender of Marxsen can put forward the point that Marxsen finally acknowledges at the end of his long expositions that even his view remain a hypothesis. This statement is formally correct. Nevertheless though, something of the whole impression remains effective, and is brought into his

154 id. p. 105.   155 id. p. 107.
156 id. p. 108.   157 id. p. 108.

further deliberations by Marxsen himself, in which he assures us, 'Therefore we do not get at what actually happened near Damascus.'[158]

This and other observations show that it is apparently only possible by means of a violent and untenable exposition of the texts to explain those sources which are in fact available in such a way as to deny the historical reality of the resurrection.

158 id. p. 109.

## Final thoughts: the significance of the historical question for theology

After one of my lectures at a meeting of German, Belgian, and Dutch theologians one of the Bible experts said to me, 'What you have worked out there is probably indisputable historically. But don't you understand the great positive intention of modern theology? It is in fact, theologically not crucial whether the tomb was found empty or not, but it is only theologically crucial that Jesus lives after his death and that his cause continues. In this sense isn't it right if modern theology says that the reports of the miracles, of the finding of the empty tomb, of the appearances of the Risen Christ are in fact only interpretaments, and that the historical sequence of events is not therefore the decisive thing, but rather that which is thereby made known to us?'

I fully agree with the fundamental concern of modern theology which is indicated by those remarks. *Yet the whole question of the historical credibility of the gospels is a matter though of the character and the weight of these symbolic interpretations.* If they are really only tales which have just been made up by some individuals or other in order to make certain statements about God, then these tales, in spite of all the grandeur which is contained within them, nevertheless have no unique and inescapable significance as 'interpretaments'. They are then only to be classified in fact with myths and poems in which there is also talk of the working of a god. They can then quite legitimately be replaced by other tales.

The matter is quite different though if these are symbolic interpretations by God himself. *If God in fact entered into history, and gave signs of His love and of His majesty, then these signs are not just any old symbolic interpretations amongst others, but they have a special quality of their own and thereby become at the same time challenging incitements which place human beings unavoidably before the decision either to believe or to withhold love and belief.*

The question of the historical credibility of the gospels is therefore from the points of view of scholarship a question which must be approached by the methods used in historical scholarship. And yet, at least to the Christian who asks this question, it is not primarily a matter of history for its own sake but a question of whether the gospels are merely documents in which people try to make certain statements about God and His works, or whether it has been correctly reported that God himself has shown his Might and his Love in these unique happenings. *With that, though, the historical question takes on decisive importance for the theologian. A theology which does not see that, or does not want to see it, demolishes the foundations from which it gets its own credibility as a Christian theology, that is to say a theology of the God who entered into history in the person of His Son.*

As has been pointed out in the course of this enquiry, the Evangelists knew that the credibility of the good tidings which they were preaching included the credible attestation of historical events. Many modern theologians seem to have forgotten this connection. They have the illusory hope of preaching the gospel more decisively by doing away with 'historical assurances', thereby awakening faith as such more purely. In fact they are like that bird who imagined that it could fly untrammelled, and higher in the heavens, without the irksome resistance of earthly air. Just like that bird, which fell back to earth when once its wish was fulfilled, so has this new theology created not a purer form of belief but a lack of faith and a falling down.

One could pursue this thought further. These theologians may be right that — considered absolutely — it can appear at first sight inappropriate to the reality of God to wish to comprehend Him by signs like the virgin birth, miracles, and resurrection, which are so clearly designed for man and his historically determined expectations.

*But: can we overcome the distance between God and ourselves, and know God as God absolutely and sufficiently? Such a supposition seems to me to include an overestimate of our possibilities. The distance between God and man can only be overcome by the obliging activity of God. That is all the more reason for joy that God did indeed come into our historical world, and set the signs which do not overtax us or our imaginations. In this is revealed at the same time that which theologians once called the humility of God. Perhaps we are suffering today from the fact that we are*

105

*only capable of answering the loving humility of God, which fits our world of imagination, with a critical intellectuality, and no longer with humility, love, and thanks.*

One last thought. If God really entered into history, then he also takes care that it is, and will be, rightly handed down. It is also credible that He ensured — and ensures — that the writings which tell of His works do not lead mankind astray, but on the chosen path. From this point of view the question of inspiration arises. In the same way as the thesis of verbal inspiration, which was formerly held by some theologians, is untenable, so is it unbelievable that God or an angel dictated their texts word for word or guided their pens, so much more compulsive is the conviction that God enters into history and gives the sign of His love, of His compassion, and of His power, in His works, His suffering, and His death and resurrection, and that He takes care that these signs should be handed down in an appropriate manner. That means that the theological credibility of the gospels goes far beyond that which can be ensured by the methods of historical research, and it means that man today as always has the right to read the Holy Scriptures with confidence as being the Word of God, without having to make himself familiar first with the present state of affairs in the scientifically conducted exegetic discussion.

106